SRA

Reading Mastery

Signature Edition

Curriculum-Based Assessment and Fluency Teacher Handbook

Grade 4

Siegfried Engelmann
Jean Osborn
Steven Osborn
Leslie Zoref

SRA

Columbus, OH

SRAonline.com

 SRA

Send all inquiries to this address:
SRA/McGraw-Hill
8787 Orion Place
Columbus, OH 43240-4027

ISBN: 978-0-07-612630-9
MHID: 0-07-612630-7

9 10 11 12 13 GLO 20 19 18 17 16

Contents

Introduction

The curriculum-based assessment and fluency system for *Reading Mastery Signature Edition,* Grade 4, is a complete system for monitoring student performance in the program. By using the curriculum-based assessment and fluency system, you can

- ensure that students are properly placed in the program
- measure student achievement within the program
- identify the skills and concepts the students have mastered
- maintain individual and group records
- administer remedial exercises

The materials for the curriculum-based assessment and fluency system consist of this Handbook and a separate Student Book for each student. The Student Book contains a placement test, a series of assessments, and passages for fluency checkouts. The Handbook contains instructions for administering the assessments and fluency checkouts, remedial exercises for each assessment, Individual Skills Profile Charts, Assessment Group Summary Charts, an Individual Fluency: Rate/ Accuracy Chart, and a Writing Assessment Chart.

The Assessments

Two kinds of assessments are used in the curriculum-based assessment and fluency system: the placement test and the mastery tests. The placement test instructions appear on page 1. The test measures the decoding and comprehension skills of students entering *Reading Mastery,* Grade 4. The test results provide guidelines for grouping students and allow you to identify students who should not be placed in the program.

The mastery tests are criterion referenced, which means they assess each student's achievement within the program. Each mastery test item measures student mastery of a specific skill or concept taught in *Reading Mastery,* Grade 4. There are twelve mastery tests, one for every ten lessons. The assessments for lessons 30, 60, 90, and 120 are

unit assessments measuring mastery of skills and concepts taught in the preceding thirty lessons.

For each mastery test, a writing prompt is included as an optional mastery test item. You may have students begin the writing assessment item while they wait for others to finish the mastery test, or you may have students complete it at another time. Evaluation guidelines for writing items begin on page 51.

The assessments measure comprehension, literary appreciation, and study skills. Decoding skills are measured by the individual fluency checkouts. For an individual fluency checkout, a student reads a passage aloud as you count decoding errors. Students earn points for reading the passage accurately. A fluency checkout takes about a minute and a half per student. The fluency checkout passages, along with further instruction, begin on page 52.

The Remedial Exercises

To pass each test, a student must answer at least 80 percent of the items correctly. The remedial exercises are designed to help students who score below 80 percent on the assessments. Each assessment has its own set of remedial exercises. The exercises provide a general review of the tested skills and concepts, using examples different from those on the test. There is a specific remedial exercise for every tested skill or concept. The remedial exercises are similar to the exercises found in the Presentation Books for *Reading Mastery,* Grade 4.

The Charts

Four charts are used in the curriculum-based assessment and fluency system: the Individual Skills Profile Chart, the Group Summary Chart, the Individual Fluency: Rate/Accuracy Chart, and the Writing Assessment Chart.

The Individual Skills Profile Chart appears on pages 66 and 67. This two-page chart lists the specific skills and concepts taught in *Reading Mastery,* Grade 4, and indicates what each assessment item measures. When the chart is completed, it shows how well a student has mastered the skills and concepts taught in *Reading Mastery,* Grade 4.

The Group Summary Chart appears on pages 68 and 69. It summarizes the group's scores on the assessments. The chart provides an objective measure of the group's progress and can be used to evaluate the group's overall performance.

The Individual Fluency: Rate/Accuracy Chart appears on page 70. This chart helps you keep track of an individual student's fluency checkout scores.

Use of Color, Bold, and Italic Type

Text is distinguished in the following ways for your convenience in administering the tests and presenting remedial exercises.

- Blue text shows what you say.
- **Bold blue text shows words you stress.**
- (Text in parentheses tells what you do.)
- *Italic text gives students' responses.* (If a student response is preceded by the word *Response,* the printed response gives the exact answer expected. If a student response is preceded by the word *Idea,* the printed response gives the general idea of a correct answer.)

PLACEMENT TEST

The placement test has two parts. In part 1, each student reads a passage aloud as you count decoding errors. In part 2, students answer comprehension questions about the passage.

Instructions for Part 1

You should administer part 1 in a corner of the classroom so that other students will not overhear the testing. Use the following procedure.

1. (Have the student look at the placement test on page 1 of the student book.)

2. (Point to the passage and say:) You're going to read the passage aloud. I want you to read it as well as you can. Don't try to read it so fast you make mistakes, but don't read it so slowly that it doesn't make any sense. You have two minutes to read the passage. Go.

3. (Time the student and make one tally mark for each error.)

4. (After two minutes, stop the student. Count every word not read as an error.)

5. (Total the student's errors.)

Use the following guidelines for counting decoding errors in part 1.

- If the student misreads a word, count one error.

- If the student omits a word ending, such as *s* or *ed*, count one error.

- If the student reads a word incorrectly and then correctly, count one error.

- If the student sounds out a word instead of reading it normally, count one error.

- If the student does not identify a word within three seconds, tell the student the word and count one error.

- If the student skips a word, count one error.

- If the student skips a line, point to the line and count one error.

- If the student does not finish the passage within the given time limit, count every word not read as an error. For example, if the student is eight words from the end of the passage at the end of the time limit, count eight errors.

Instructions for Part 2

After all the students have finished part 1, administer part 2 to the entire group. Use the following procedure.

1. (Assemble the students.)

2. (Tell the students to look at page 1 of the student book.)

3. (Say:) Here is the passage you read earlier. Read the passage again silently; then answer the questions in part 2. You have seven minutes. Go.

4. (Collect the student books after seven minutes.)

5. (Total each student's errors, using the answer key below.)

Answer Key for Part 2

1. Idea: *the Bermuda Islands*

2. Ideas: *to dive; to see the bottom of the ocean*

3. Response: *warm*

4. Response: *the guide*

5. Ideas: *partner; person*

6. Idea: *Signal the guide.*

7. Idea: *Go to the surface of the water.*

8. Idea: *The diver might get the bends.*

9. Response: *pressure*

Placement Guidelines

Place your students as follows:

- Students who made zero errors or one error should be given the placement test for *Reading Mastery,* Grade 5.

- Students who made zero to six errors on part 1 *and* zero to two errors on part 2 can be placed in *Reading Mastery,* Grade 4.

- Students who made more than six errors on part 1 or more than two errors on part 2 should be given the placement test for *Reading Mastery,* Grade 3.

A reproducible copy of the placement test appears on page 72.

Mastery Tests/Assessments

LESSON 10

Administering the Assessment

The Lesson 10 Mastery Test should be administered after the students complete all work on lesson 10 and before they begin work on lesson 11. Each student will need a pencil and a copy of the *Curriculum-Based Assessment and Fluency Student Book.* Use the following procedure.

1. (Have the students clear their desks. Make sure each student has a pencil.)

2. Now you're going to take a short test on what you've learned. Don't begin until I tell you.

3. Write your name on the name line at the top of the page.

4. Look at the sample items. I'll read the first sample item.
   For item 1, circle the letter of the answer that means the same thing as the underlined part.
       1. Ron was sitting on a <u>large rock</u>.
         a. boulder
         b. poster
         c. brook

5. What is the correct answer? (Response: *Boulder.*)
   - Everybody, circle the letter for that answer.
   - What letter did you circle? (Response: *A.*)

6. I'll read the next sample item.
   For item 2, circle the letter of the correct answer.
       2. Where does Dorothy live?
         a. Kentucky
         b. Arkansas
         c. Kansas

7. What is the correct answer? (Response: *Kansas.*)
   - Everybody, circle the letter for that answer.
   - What letter did you circle? (Response: *C.*) (Make sure all students have circled the letters correctly.)

8. You will answer all the items on the test just as you answered these sample items. For some items, you must circle the letter of the answer that means the same thing as the underlined part. For other items, you must circle the letter of the correct answer.

9. Now you're ready to begin the test. Answer all the items on both pages. For each item, you must circle the letter of the correct answer. There is no time limit. When you've finished, turn your test facedown and look up at me. Begin the test now. (If you are including the writing item as part of the testing session, tell students they can begin the writing item after they finish the mastery test.)

Grading the Mastery Test

You can grade the tests yourself, or you can have the students grade their own tests. If you want the students to grade their own tests, use the following procedure.

1. Now we're going to grade the test. I'll read the correct answer for each item. If the answer is correct, mark it with a **C.** If the answer is wrong, mark it with an **X.**

2. (Read the correct answers from the answer key on pages 7 and 8.)

3. Now count the number of **correct** answers and enter the score at the end of the test.

Answer Key

Lesson 10

1. a		10. b	
2. c		11. a	
3. b		12. c	
4. c		13. a	
5. b		14. b	
6. a		15. c	
7. c		16. b	
8. b		17. a	
9. c		18. c	

Recording Individual Results

The students record their test results on the Individual Skills Profile Chart. Use the following procedure to explain the chart.

1. (Give each student a copy of the appropriate chart. Tell students to write their names on the name line at the upper right.)

2. This is your Individual Skills Profile Chart. Look at the left side of the chart. The words on the left side tell about the reading skills you're learning.

3. Look at the top line of the chart. The numbers on the top line are lesson numbers.
- What is the first number? (Response: *10.*)
- What is the last number? (Response: *60.*) You will take a test for each of the lesson numbers. When we finish lesson 60, I'll give you another sheet with numbers for lessons 70 through 120. You have just finished the test for lesson 10.

4. Now look at the column of numbers under lesson 10. Those numbers tell about the items on the test for lesson 10.
- What is the first number in the column? (Response: *1.*)
That number tells about test item number 1. Now look **down** the column.
- What is the last number in the column? (Response: *12.*)
- What test item does that number tell about? (Response: *Item 12.*)
You can see that the order of the numbers is not the same in every column.

5. Now I'll tell you how to record your test results on the chart. First, look at the test to find out which items you got wrong. Then circle those numbers on the chart.
- Which number would you circle if you got number 2 wrong? (Response: *2.*)

6. Now record your results. I'll help you if you have questions. (Circulate among the students as they record their results.)

7. (After the students finish, say:) Now count the items you did **not** circle and write the total in the **Total** box near the bottom of the column. The total should be the same as your test score.

8. Below the **Total** box is the **Retest** box. If you scored 0 to 14 points, write an **X** in the **Retest** box. Below the **Retest** box is the **FINAL SCORE** box. If you scored 15 to 18 points, write your score in the **FINAL SCORE** box.

Remedial Exercises

Students who scored 0 to 14 points on the test should be given remedial help. After the regular reading period is over, assemble these students and present the following exercises. The students will need their original test papers.

EXERCISE 1   Vocabulary Review

1. Let's talk about the meanings of some words.

2. The first word is **dangerous.** When something is **dangerous,** it is unsafe.
- Everybody, what's another way of saying **The path is unsafe?** (Signal.) *The path is dangerous.*

3. The next word is **kayak.** Someone who is paddling a small canoe is paddling a **kayak.**
- Everybody, what's another way of saying **She was paddling the small canoe down the river?** (Signal.) *She was paddling the kayak down the river.*

4. The next word is **startled.** Someone who is surprised is **startled.**
- Everybody, what's another way of saying **She was surprised?** (Signal.) *She was startled.*

5. The next word is **disappeared.** Something that has vanished has **disappeared.**
- Everybody, what's another way of saying **The boy has vanished?** (Signal.) *The boy has disappeared.*

6. The next word is **gorgeous.** When something is **gorgeous,** it is very pretty.
- Everybody, what's another way of saying **The colors were very pretty?** (Signal.) *The colors were gorgeous.*

7. The next word is **solemn. Solemn** is another word for **serious.**
- Everybody, what's another way of saying **The ceremony was serious?** (Signal.) *The ceremony was solemn.*

8. The next word is **injured. Injured** is another word for **hurt.**
- Everybody, what's another way of saying **The cat hurt its leg?** (Signal.) *The cat injuredits leg.*

9. The next word is **dismally. Dismally** is another word for **sadly.**
- Everybody, what's another way of saying **The dog howled dismally?** (Signal.) *The dog howled sadly.*

10. The next word is **ripples. Ripples** are small waves.
- Everybody, what's another way of saying **The small waves spread across the lake?** (Signal.) *The ripples spread across the lake.*

11. The next word is **cradle. Cradle** is another word for **small bed.**
- Everybody, what's another way of saying **The baby slept in a small bed?** (Signal.) *The baby slept in a cradle.*

12. The next word is **merrily. Merrily** is another word for **happily.**
- Everybody, what's another way of saying **The boats went merrily down the stream?** (Signal.) *The boats went happily down the stream.*

13. The last word is **boulder.** A **boulder** is a **large rock.**
- Everybody, what's another way of saying **Tom saw a large rock?** (Signal.) *Tom saw a boulder.*

EXERCISE 2   *General Review*

1. Chapter 3 of *The Wonderful Wizard of Oz* is called "The Munchkins." What main thing does that chapter tell about? (Idea: *The Munchkins.*)

2. What is the strong wind called that blew Dorothy's house to the Land of the Munchkins? (Response: A *cyclone.*)

3. What color was the Emerald City? (Response: *Green.*)

4. What was the name of the people who wore blue clothes? (Response: *The Munchkins.*)

5. Did Dorothy meet the Scarecrow **before** or **after** she started out on the yellow brick road? (Response: *After.*)

6. Did Dorothy's house land on a witch **before** or **after** Dorothy saw a cyclone coming? (Response: *After.*)

7. Pretend you want to look up the word **current** in your glossary.
- What letter does **current** start with? (Response: *C.*)
- So what letter would you look under? (Response: *C.*)

8. What direction is always at the top of a map? (Response: *North.*)

9. What direction is always on the left side of a map? (Response: *West.*)

10. Pretend you are in the Land of the South. What direction would you go to get to the Land of the North? (Response: *North.*)

11. Pretend you are in the Land of the East. What direction would you go to get to the Land of the West? (Response: *West.*)

1. Everybody, look at the passage on page 3 of your test. You're going to read the passage aloud.

2. (Call on individual students to read several sentences each. Correct all decoding errors. When the students finish, present the following questions.)

3. Where are rapids found? (Idea: *In a river.*)

4. Why was Ron frightened? (Idea: *Rapids are fast and have boulders.*)

5. How did Ron try to move the kayak to the right? (Idea: *By paddling on the left.*)

6. Why did Ron have a hard time turning the kayak? (Idea: *Because the current was strong and fast.*)

7. What playground ride did the rapids remind him of? (Idea: *A slide.*)

8. What do you think Ron will do next? (Ideas: *Try to get out of the rapids; get into an accident.*)

9. How hard will Ron probably have to paddle if he comes to another boulder? (Idea: *Very hard.*)

10. What title would you give this passage? (Ideas: *Ron in the Rapids; Ron in Trouble.*)

11. Did the rapids get better or worse? (Response: *Worse.*)

Retesting the Students

After you've completed the remedial exercises, retest each student individually. To administer the retest, you will need the student's original test paper, a blank copy of the test, and a red pencil. Test the student in a corner of the classroom so that the other students will not overhear the testing. Give the student the blank copy of the test. Say, "Look at page 2. You're going to take this test again. Read each item aloud and tell me the answer."

Use the student's original test paper to grade the retest. Use the red pencil to mark each correct answer with a **C** and each incorrect answer with an **X.** Then count one point for each correct answer and

write the new score at the bottom of the page. Finally, revise the Individual Skills Profile Chart by drawing an **X** over any items the student missed on the retest. The chart should now show which items the student missed on the initial test and which items the student missed on the retest.
Page 65 shows a partially completed Individual Skills Profile Chart.

Recording Group Results

After the students have completely filled in the Individual Skills Profile Chart for lesson 10, you should fill in the Group Summary Chart, which appears on page 68. Make a copy of the chart and then enter the students' names on the left side of the chart under the heading "Names." Record the students' scores in the boxes under the appropriate lesson number. Highlight any score below 80%.

Fluency: Rate/Accuracy

Administer the fluency checkout for lesson 10. The passage begins on page 53. For further instructions, see page 52.

Tested Skills and Concepts

The Lesson 10 Mastery Test measures student mastery of the following skills.

- using vocabulary words in context (items 1–3)
- using context to predict word meaning (items 4–6)
- identifying literal cause and effect (item 7)
- distinguishing settings by features (item 8)
- sequencing narrative events (item 9)
- interpreting a character's feelings (item 10)
- interpreting maps (items 11, 12)
- answering literal questions about a text (item 13)
- inferring cause and effect (item 14)
- evaluating problems and solutions (item 15)
- predicting narrative outcomes (item 16)
- predicting a character's actions (item 17)
- relating titles to story content (item 18)

LESSON 20

Administering the Test

The Lesson 20 Mastery Test should be administered after the students complete all work on lesson 20 and before they begin work on lesson 21. Each student will need a pencil and a copy of the *Curriculum-Based Assessment and Fluency Student Book.* Use the following script.

1. (Have the students clear their desks. Make sure each student has a pencil.)

2. Now you're going to take another test on what you've learned. Don't begin until I tell you.

3. Write your name on the name line on the top of the page.

4. Now you're ready to begin the test. Answer all the items on both pages. There is no time limit. When you've finished, turn your test facedown and look up at me. Begin the test now. (If you are including the writing item as part of the testing session, tell students they can begin the writing item after they finish the mastery test.)

Grading the Test

You can grade the tests yourself, or you can have the students grade their own tests. If you want the students to grade their own tests, use the following procedure.

1. Now we're going to grade the test. I'll read the correct answer for each item. If the answer is correct, mark it with a **C.** If the answer is wrong, mark it with an **X.**

2. (Read the correct answers from the answer key in the next column.)

3. Now count the number of correct answers and enter the score at the end of the test.

Answer Key

LESSON 20

Name _____

For items 1–6, circle the letter of the answer that means the same thing as the underlined part.

1. Please let in the customers with tickets.
   - (a.) admit
   - b. prefer
   - c. spoil

2. The dog was a loyal friend.
   - a. coward
   - (b.) comrade
   - c. mistress

3. The shy man did not dare to speak.
   - a. deserted
   - (b.) timid
   - c. gloomy

4. The fortunate boy found a dollar on the street.
   - a. civilized
   - b. awkward
   - (c.) lucky

5. Everyone was astonished when the cat began to speak.
   - a. injured
   - (b.) surprised
   - c. prepared

6. Her delightful cookies cheered up the patient.
   - (a.) wonderful
   - b. frosted
   - c. decorated

For items 7–18, circle the letter of the correct answer.

7. What did the Tin Woodman want from Oz?
   - a. Courage
   - (b.) A heart
   - c. Brains

8. What color was Kansas?
   - (a.) Gray
   - b. Green
   - c. Brown

9. Which character was never hungry?
   - (a.) The Scarecrow
   - b. Dorothy
   - c. Toto

10. Which character didn't think he ever had any good ideas?
    - a. The Tin Woodman
    - b. The Lion
    - (c.) The Scarecrow

11. What wall was a bright green color?
    - a. The wall along the yellow brick road
    - (b.) The wall around the Emerald City
    - c. The wall around the field of flowers

12. Which event could only happen in a story?
    - (a.) A girl visits the Land of Oz.
    - b. A girl visits Kansas.
    - c. A girl reads a book.

Read the passage below. Then answer items 13–18.

The travelers walked along listening to the singing of the bright-colored birds and looking at the lovely flowers, which now became so thick that the ground was covered with them.

"Aren't they beautiful?" Dorothy asked as she breathed in the spicy scent of the flowers.

"I always did like flowers," said the Lion. "They seem so helpless. But there are none in the forest as bright as these."

Now, when there are many of these scarlet flowers together, their odor is so powerful that anyone who breathes them falls asleep; and if the sleeper is not carried away from the flowers, he sleeps on forever. But Dorothy did not know this, nor could she get away from the flowers.

Her eyes soon grew heavy, and she felt she must sit down to rest and sleep.

But the Tin Woodman would not let her do this.

"We must hurry and get back to the yellow brick road before dark," he said. So they kept walking until Dorothy could stand no longer. Her eyes closed, and she forgot where she was, and she fell among the flowers, fast asleep.

"What shall we do?" asked the Tin Woodman.

"If we leave her here, she will die," said the Lion. "The smell of the flowers is killing us all. I can scarcely keep my eyes open, and the dog is asleep already."

It was true—Toto had fallen down beside his mistress. But the Scarecrow and the Tin Woodman, since they weren't made of flesh, were not troubled by the odor of the flowers.

13. The passage is from one of the chapters of *The Wonderful Wizard of Oz.* What do you think the title of the chapter is?
    - (a.) "The Field of Flowers"
    - b. "The River"
    - c. "The Field Mice"

14. Why was the Lion able to stay awake longer than Dorothy?
    - (a.) He was bigger and stronger.
    - b. He was not made of flesh.
    - c. He was shorter.

15. How was Dorothy different from the Scarecrow?
    - a. Dorothy heard the birds singing.
    - b. Dorothy saw the flowers.
    - (c.) Dorothy was made of flesh and blood.

16. Which one of the following things would be troubled by the odor of the flowers?
    - a. A stuffed cat
    - (b.) A brown cow
    - c. A wooden horse

17. Why did the Lion like the flowers?
    - (a.) They seemed so helpless.
    - b. They had a strong odor.
    - c. They were scarlet.

18. Which character might say, "I like these flowers because they are very pretty"?
    - a. The Tin Woodman
    - b. The Scarecrow
    - (c.) Dorothy

STOP—end of test—SCORE: _____

Recording Individual Results

(Use the following script to record individual results.)

1. Look at your Individual Skills Profile Chart.

2. You're going to record your test results for lesson 20. First look at the test to find out which items you got wrong. Then circle those items on the chart.

3. Now record your results. I'll help you if you have any questions. (Circulate among the students as they record their results.)

4. (After the students finish, say:) Now count the items you did *not* circle and write the total in the *Total* box near the bottom of the column. The total should be the same as your test score.

5. Now you'll fill in the other boxes for lesson 20. If you scored 0 to 14 points, write an **X** in the box marked **Retest.** If you scored 15 to 18 points, write your score in the box marked **FINAL SCORE.**

Remedial Exercises

Students who scored 0 to 14 points on the test should be given remedial help. After the regular reading period is over, assemble these students and present the following exercises. The students will need their original test papers.

| EXERCISE 1 | Vocabulary Review |

1. Let's talk about the meanings of some words.

2. The first word is **fortunate.** When you are **fortunate,** you are lucky.
- Everybody, what's another way of saying **The man felt lucky to be alive?** (Signal.) *The man felt fortunate to be alive.*

3. The next word is **awkward.** Someone who is clumsy is **awkward.**
- Everybody, what's another way of saying **She was so clumsy that she kept falling down?** (Signal.) *She was so awkward that she kept falling down.*

4. The next word is **timid.** Someone who is very shy is **timid.**
- Everybody, what's another way of saying **She was very shy?** (Signal.) *She was timid.*

5. The next word is **admit.** When you **admit** someone to a place, you let that person come in.
- Everybody, what's another way of saying **The guard let them come in?** (Signal.) *The guard admitted them.*

6. The next word is **astonished. Astonished** is another word for **surprised.**
- Everybody, what's another way of saying **The magician surprised the crowd?** (Signal.) *The magician astonished the crowd.*

7. The next word is **scarcely.** If you can **scarcely** do something, you can hardly do it.
- Everybody, what's another way of saying **The baby could hardly walk?** (Signal.) *The baby could scarcely walk.*

8. The next word is **comrade.** A **comrade** is a friend.
- Everybody, what's another way of saying **Tom was his best friend?** (Signal.) *Tom was his best comrade.*

9. The next word is **delightful. Delightful** is another word for **wonderful.**
- Everybody, what's another way of saying **The weather was wonderful?** (Signal.) *The weather was delightful.*

10. The next word is **declared. Declared** is another word for **said.**
- Everybody, what's another way of saying **The teacher said it was a holiday?** (Signal.) *The teacher declared it was a holiday.*

11. The next word is **sorrow. Sorrow** is another word for **sadness.**
- Everybody, what's another way of saying **The bad news filled her with sadness?** (Signal.) *The bad news filled her with sorrow.*

12. The next word is **scarlet. Scarlet** is another word for **bright red.**
- Everybody, what's another way of saying **The bullfighter's cape was bright red?** (Signal.) *The bullfighter's cape was scarlet.*

13. The last word is **glittered. Glittered** is another word for **sparkled.**
- Everybody, what's another way of saying **The diamonds sparkled?** (Signal.) *The diamonds glittered.*

EXERCISE 2 — General Review

1. Which character wanted a heart? (Response: *The Tin Woodman.*)

2. What color did the Munchkins paint the Scarecrow's eyes? (Response: *Blue.*)

3. Chapter 13 of *The Wonderful Wizard of Oz* is called "The Field Mice." What is the main thing the chapter tells about? (Idea: *The field mice.*)

4. Why did the Tin Woodman get rusty? (Idea: *He got caught in a rainstorm.*)

5. What was the name of the cowardly character? (Idea: *The Cowardly Lion.*)

6. How did the characters get across the ditch? (Idea: *They sat on the Lion's back, and he jumped across.*)

7. Which characters never ate anything? (Ideas: *The Scarecrow and the Tin Woodman.*)

8. What was the gate of the Emerald City studded with? (Response: *Emeralds.*)

9. Pretend you want to look up the word **comrade** in your glossary.
   • What letter does **comrade** start with? (Response: *C.*)
   • So what letter would you look under? (Response: *C.*)

EXERCISE 3 — Passage Reading

1. Everybody, look at the passage on page 6 of your test. You're going to read the passage aloud.

2. (Call on individual students to read several sentences each. Correct all decoding errors. When the students finish, present the following questions.)

3. Who was stronger, Dorothy or the Lion? (Response: *The Lion.*)

4. So who could jump farther, Dorothy or the Lion? (Response: *The Lion.*)

5. Name some ways the Lion was different from the Tin Woodman. (Ideas: *The Lion was made of flesh; the Lion had fur; the Lion had to sleep.*)

6. Things that are not made of flesh and blood don't have to sleep. So which characters did not have to sleep? (Ideas: *The Tin Woodman; the Scarecrow.*)

7. Why was the Lion afraid of things that could fight him? (Idea: *He was a coward.*)

8. So what kinds of things would the Lion like? (Idea: *Things that could not fight him.*)

9. Which character might say, "I don't have the heart to love these flowers"? (Response: *The Tin Woodman.*)

Retesting the Students

After you've completed the remedial exercises, retest each student individually. To administer the retest, you will need the student's original test paper, a blank copy of the test, and a red pencil. Give the student the blank copy of the test. Say, "Look at page 5. You're going to take this test again. Read each item aloud and tell me the answer."

Use the student's original test paper to grade the retest. Use the red pencil to mark each correct answer with a **C** and each incorrect answer with an **X**. Then count one point for each correct answer and write the new score at the bottom of the page. Finally, revise the Individual Skills Profile Chart by drawing an **X** over any items the student missed on the retest.

Fluency: Rate/Accuracy

Administer the fluency checkout for lesson 20. The passage begins on page 54. For further instructions, see page 52.

Tested Skills

The following list shows the test items and the skills they test.
• using vocabulary words in context (items 1–3)
• using context to predict word meaning (items 4–6)
• interpreting a character's motives (item 7)
• distinguishing characters by trait (items 9 and 10)
• distinguishing settings by features (items 8 and 11)
• distinguishing between fact and fiction (item 12)
• relating titles to story content (item 13)
• inferring cause and effect (item 14)
• making comparisons (item 15)
• drawing conclusions (item 16)
• inferring a character's point of view (item 17)
• interpreting a character's feelings (item 18)

LESSON 30

Administering the Test

The Lesson 30 Mastery Test should be administered after the students complete all work on lesson 30 and before they begin work on lesson 31. Each student will need a pencil and a copy of the *Curriculum-Based Assessment and Fluency Student Book*. Use the following script.

1. (Have the students clear their desks. Make sure each student has a pencil.)

2. Now you're going to take another test on what you've learned. This test will be longer than the others you've taken because it has questions about the last thirty lessons. Don't begin until I tell you.

3. Write your name on the name line.

4. Now you're ready to begin the test. Answer all the items on each page. There is no time limit. When you've finished, turn your test facedown and look up at me. Begin the test now. (If you are including the writing item as part of the testing session, tell students they can begin the writing item after they finish the mastery test.)

Grading the Test

You can grade the tests yourself, or you can have the students grade their own tests. If you want the students to grade their own tests, use the following procedure.

1. Now we're going to grade the test. I'll read the correct answer for each item. If the answer is correct, mark it with a **C.** If the answer is wrong, mark it with an **X.**

2. (Read the correct answers from the answer key on these two pages.)

3. Now count the number of correct answers and enter the score at the end of the test.

Answer Key

Lesson 30

1.	c	25.	a
2.	a	26.	c
3.	b	27.	b
4.	a	28.	a
5.	b	29.	c
6.	a	30.	b
7.	c	31.	a
8.	a	32.	b
9.	b	33.	c
10.	a	34.	a
11.	c	35.	c
12.	a	36.	a
13.	b	37.	c
14.	a	38.	b
15.	c	39.	c
16.	b	40.	b
17.	a	41.	a
18.	b	42.	c
19.	c	43.	b
20.	a	44.	c
21.	b	45.	b
22.	a	46.	a
23.	c	47.	b
24.	b	48.	c

Recording Individual Results

(Use the following script to record individual results.)

1. Look at your Individual Skills Profile Chart.

2. You're going to record your test results for lesson 30. First look at the test to find out which items you got wrong. Then circle those items on the chart.

3. Now record your results. I'll help you if you have any questions. (Circulate among the students as they record their results.)

4. (After the students finish, say:) Now count the items you did not circle and write the total in the **Total** box near the bottom of the column. The total should be the same as your test score.

5. Now you'll fill in the other boxes for lesson 30. If you scored 0 to 38 points, write an **X** in the box marked **Retest.** If you scored 39 to 48 points, write your score in the box marked **FINAL SCORE.**

Remedial Exercises

Students who scored 0 to 38 points on the test should be given remedial help. After the regular reading period is over, assemble these students and present the following exercises. The students will need their original test papers.

EXERCISE 1   Vocabulary Review

1. Let's talk about the meanings of some words.

2. The first word is **wail. Wail** is another word for **howl.**
- Everybody, what's another way of saying **Did you hear the wind howl last night?** (Signal.) *Did you hear the wind wail last night?*

3. The next word is **brilliant.** Something that is bright and colorful is **brilliant.**
- Everybody, what's another way of saying **The gems were bright and colorful?** (Signal.) *The gems were brilliant.*

4. The next word is **messenger.** A **messenger** is a person who delivers messages.
- Everybody, what's another way of saying **I saw the person who delivers messages?** (Signal.) *I saw the messenger.*

5. The next word is **clumsiness. Clumsiness** is another word for **awkwardness.**

- Everybody, what's another way of saying **His awkwardness was sometimes dangerous?** (Signal.) *His clumsiness was sometimes dangerous.*

6. The next word is **misfortune. Misfortune** means "bad luck."
- Everybody, what's another way of saying **I'm sorry about your bad luck?** (Signal.) *I'm sorry about your misfortune.*

7. The next word is **dazzle. Dazzle** is another word for **amaze.**
- Everybody, what's another way of saying **The diamonds amazed them?** (Signal.) *The diamonds dazzled them.*

8. The next word is **slightest. Slightest** is another word for **smallest.**
- Everybody, what's another way of saying **He gave us the smallest wave?** (Signal.) *He gave us the slightest wave.*

9. The next word is **feast.** A **feast** is a large meal.
- Everybody, what's another way of saying **We enjoyed the large meal?** (Signal.) *We enjoyed the feast.*

10. The next word is **reunited. Reunited** means "put together again."
- Everybody, what's another way of saying **The sisters were put together again?** (Signal.) *The sisters were reunited.*

11. The next word is **promptly.** If you do something **promptly,** you do it on time.
- Everybody, what's another way of saying **Turn in your test on time?** (Signal.) *Turn in your test promptly.*

12. The next word is **consider.** To **consider** something is to think it over.
- Everybody, what's another way of saying **You should think over big decisions?** (Signal.) *You should consider big decisions.*

13. The next word is **uneasy.** When you are **uneasy** about something, you are uncomfortable about it.
- Everybody, what's another way of saying **She was uncomfortable about her essay?** (Signal.) *She was uneasy about her essay.*

14. The next word is **utter. Utter** is another word for **say.**
- Everybody, what's another way of saying **The boy uttered his name?** (Signal.) *The boy said his name.*

EXERCISE 2   General Review

1. Where did Dorothy live? (Response: *Kansas.*)

2. Where did Dorothy and Aunt Em go when the cyclone came? (Response: *To the cellar.*)

3. Chapter 4 of *The Wonderful Wizard of Oz* is called "The Yellow Brick Road." What main thing does that chapter tell about? (Response: *The yellow brick road.*)

4. Whom did Dorothy's house land on? (Idea: *The Wicked Witch of the East.*)

5. Who ruled the Emerald City? (Idea: *Oz.*)

6. Which character had straw for brains? (Response: *The Scarecrow.*)

7. Who made the Scarecrow? (Idea: *The Munchkins.*)

8. How long had the Tin Woodman been rusted? (Idea: *More than a year.*)

9. Why did the Tin Woodman want a heart? (Idea: *So he could marry the Munchkin maiden.*)

10. What did the Lion want from Oz? (Idea: *Courage.*)

11. Who chopped down the tree so the travelers could walk across the ditch? (Response: *The Tin Woodman.*)

12. Who plucked the Scarecrow from the river? (Response: *The stork.*)

13. What place looked all green? (Idea: *The Emerald City.*)

14. What was floating on the throne? (Idea: *A head.*)

15. Whom did Oz want Dorothy to kill? (Idea: *The Wicked Witch of the West.*)

16. Who carried Dorothy to the witch? (Idea: *The Winged Monkeys.*)

17. Did Dorothy throw the water on the witch **before** or **after** she met Glinda? (Response: *Before.*)

18. What did Oz call himself? (Idea: *A humbug.*)

19. How did Oz leave the Emerald City?(Idea: *In a balloon.*)

20. How many commands did the golden cap give each owner? (Response: *Three.*)

21. Pretend you want to look up the word **instead** in the glossary.
- What letter does **instead** start with? (Response: *I.*)
- What letter would you look under? (Response: *I.*)

22. Which direction is always at the bottom of a map? (Response: *South.*)

23. Which direction is always on the right side of a map? (Response: *East.*)

24. Pretend you are in the Land of the North. What direction would you go to get to the Land of the South? (Response: *South.*)

25. Pretend you are in the Land of the West. What direction would you go to get to the Land of the East? (Response: *East.*)

EXERCISE 3   Passage Reading

Passage 1

1. Everybody, look at the first passage on page 9 of your test. You're going to read the passage aloud.

2. (Call on individual students to read several sentences each. Correct all decoding errors. When the students finish, present the following questions.)

3. At the beginning of the passage, what did Ron hear? (Idea: *Roaring rapids.*)

4. Why couldn't he see them? (Idea: *A bend in the river blocked his view.*)

5. How did Ron feel about the sound of the rapids? (Idea: *He was afraid.*)

6. What supplies did Ron have? (Idea: *None.*)

7. Why was Ron glad he didn't have any supplies? (Idea: *Nothing would get wet or lost if the kayak tipped over.*)

8. Why was Ron worried about having no supplies? (Idea: *He might get hungry or lost; he would have no light and no place to sleep; he might encounter bears.*)

Passage 2

1. Everybody, look at the second passage on page 10 of your test. You're going to read the passage aloud.

2. (Call on individual students to read several sentences each. Correct all decoding errors. When the students finish, present the following questions.)

3. At the beginning of the passage, what was the scenery like? (Ideas: *There were no fences; there were no farms.*)

4. Then what did Dorothy and the Scarecrow come to? (Idea: *A great forest.*)

5. Were the trees in the forest big or little? (Response: *Big.*)

6. How big were the trees? (Ideas: *Their branches met over the road; they shut out the daylight.*)

7. Where did the Scarecrow say the Emerald City was? (Idea: *At the end of the road.*)

8. Did the Scarecrow think he was smart for figuring that out? (Response: *No.*)
Why not? (Idea: *As Dorothy said, "Anyone would know about the road."*)

9. How could Toto see in the dark, although Dorothy couldn't? (Idea: *Some dogs see very well in the dark.*)

Passage 3

1. Everybody, look at the passage on page 11 of your test. You're going to read the passage aloud.

2. (Call on individual students to read several sentences each. Correct all decoding errors. When the students finish, present the following questions.)

3. What did Dorothy call Oz? (Idea: *A very bad man.*)

4. What did Oz call himself? (Idea: *A very good man but a very bad wizard.*)

5. What did the Scarecrow ask Oz for? (Idea: *Brains.*)

6. What did Oz tell the Scarecrow he was learning every day? (Idea: *Something.*)

7. What brings knowledge? (Idea: *Experience.*)

8. Where did Oz tell the Scarecrow he would stuff brains into? (Idea: *The Scarecrow's head.*)

9. What did Oz tell the Scarecrow he would have to find out for himself? (Idea: *How to use the brains.*)

Retesting the Students

After you've completed the remedial exercises, retest each student individually. To administer the retest, you will need the student's original test paper, a blank copy of the test, and a red pencil. Give the student the blank copy of the test. Say, "Look at page 8. You're going to take this test again. Read each item aloud and tell me the answer."

Use the student's original test paper to grade the retest. Use the red pencil to mark each correct answer with a **C** and each incorrect answer with an **X**. Then count one point for each correct answer and write the new score at the bottom of the page. Finally, revise the Individual Skills Profile Chart by drawing an **X** over any items the student missed on the retest.

Fluency: Rate/Accuracy

Administer the fluency checkout for lesson 30. The passage begins on page 55. For further instructions, see page 52.

Tested Skills

The following list shows the test items and the skills they test.

- using vocabulary words in context (items 1–6)
- using context to predict word meaning (items 7–12)
- recalling details and events (items 13, 22, 36)
- identifying literal cause and effect (items 14 and 34)
- sequencing narrative events (items 15 and 35)
- distinguishing settings by features (items 16 and 37)
- answering literal questions about a text (items 17 and 44)
- predicting narrative outcomes (items 18 and 47)
- inferring cause and effect (items 19, 28, and 30)
- interpreting a character's feelings (items 20 and 33)
- evaluating problems and solutions (item 21)
- interpreting glossaries (items 23 and 41)
- making comparisons (items 24 and 31)
- distinguishing characters by traits (items 25 and 38)
- relating titles to story content (items 26 and 45)
- inferring a character's point of view (item 27)
- predicting a character's actions (item 29)
- interpreting a character's motives (items 32 and 46)
- interpreting maps (items 39 and 40)
- distinguishing between fact and fiction (item 42)
- inferring story details and events (item 43)
- drawing conclusions (item 48)

LESSON 40

Administering the Test

The Lesson 40 Mastery Test should be administered after the students complete all work on lesson 40 and before they begin work on lesson 41. Each student will need a pencil and a copy of the *Curriculum-Based Assessment and Fluency Student Book.* Use the following script.

1. (Have the students clear their desks. Make sure each student has a pencil.)

2. Now you're going to take another test on what you've learned. Don't begin until I tell you.

3. Write your name on the name line.

4. Now you're ready to begin the test. Answer all the items on both pages. There is no time limit. When you've finished, turn your test facedown and look up at me. Begin the test now. (If you are including the writing item as part of the testing session, tell students they can begin the writing item after they finish the mastery test.)

Grading the Test

You can grade the test yourself, or you can have the students grade their own tests. If you want the students to grade their own tests, use the following script.

1. Now we're going to grade the test. I'll read the correct answer for each item. If the answer is correct, mark it with a **C.** If the answer is wrong, mark it with an **X.**

2. (Read the correct answers from the answer key in the next column.)

3. Now count the number of **correct** answers and enter the score at the end of the test.

Answer Key

LESSON 40

Name _____

For items 1–6, circle the letter of the answer that means the same thing as the underlined part.

1. I got this underline{black and blue mark} on my arm when I fell off my bike.
   a. bruise ✓
   b. reflection
   c. nudge

2. That underline{broken-down} car should be towed away.
   a. chattering
   b. dilapidated ✓
   c. disgusting

3. The runner was underline{making his body work as hard as it could} to reach the finish line first.
   a. lagging behind
   b. straining ✓
   c. dangling

4. The dog gave the ball a underline{nudge}, and the ball rolled away.
   a. gentle push ✓
   b. loud bark
   c. hard stare

5. The underline{pasture} is full of flowers at this time of year.
   a. person who works at a church
   b. field for farm animals ✓
   c. park area with swings

6. The trainer is working with a beautiful new underline{Thoroughbred}.
   a. special breed of racehorse ✓
   b. old, broken-down horse
   c. small pony used for children's rides

For items 7–18, circle the letter of the correct answer.

7. Where does the story "A Horse to Remember" take place?
   a. Kansas
   b. England ✓
   c. Kenya

8. At the beginning of "A Horse to Remember," what was the problem with Nellie?
   a. She had tiny black spots.
   b. She went out in a rainstorm.
   c. She kept jumping over fences. ✓

9. When a horse jumps up, the horse's rider can fall backward. So what should the rider do when the horse jumps up?
   a. The rider should lean forward. ✓
   b. The rider should lean backward.
   c. The rider should lean sideways.

10. Why did Tara train Nellie to become a steeplechase horse?
    a. Tara wanted to sell Nellie.
    b. Tara wanted to keep Nellie. ✓
    c. Tara wanted to stay home from school.

Look at the encyclopedia index below. Then answer items 11 and 12.

Article	Book—Page
Grand Canyon	17—342
Grant, Ulysses S.	8—168
Grape	9—27
Graphic Arts	14—461

11. Which book has an article on a type of fruit?
    a. 8
    b. 9 ✓
    c. 14

12. On what page will you find the article about Ulysses S. Grant?
    a. 21
    b. 168 ✓
    c. 342

Read the passage below. Then answer items 13–18.

Later that day, the mother and her ducklings went down to a clearing by the river. Some full-grown ducks were swimming in the river, and others were waddling around and quacking in chorus.

One large duck quacked much louder than the rest, and when he saw the ugly duckling, he said, in a voice that seemed to echo, "I have never seen anything as ugly as that great tall duckling. He is a disgrace. I shall go and chase him away." And he ran up to the brown duckling and bit his neck, making a small bruise.

The ugly duckling gave out a loud quack because this was the first time he had felt any pain. His mother turned around quickly.

"Leave him alone," she said fiercely to the loud duck. "What has he done to you?"

"Nothing," answered the duck. "He is just so disgusting that I can't stand him!"

Although the ugly duckling did not understand the meaning of the loud duck's words, he felt he was being blamed for something. He became even more uncomfortable when the loud duck said, "It certainly is a great shame that he is so different from the rest of us. Too bad he can't be hatched again."

The poor little fellow dropped his head and did not know what to do, but he was comforted when his mother answered, "He may not be quite as handsome as the others, but he swims with ease, and he is very strong. I am sure he will make his way in the world as well as anybody."

"I doubt it," said the loud duck as he waddled off.

13. Why did the duckling begin to quack?
    a. He felt pain. ✓
    b. The other ducks were quacking in chorus.
    c. He was arguing with the loud duck.

14. What will probably happen if the duckling visits the other ducks again?
    a. The duckling will feel welcome.
    b. The duckling will feel unwelcome. ✓
    c. The duckling will turn into a swan.

15. Where does this scene take place?
    a. In a clearing ✓
    b. On a river
    c. Beside the duckling's nest

16. Which character was cruel and unfriendly?
    a. The loud duck ✓
    b. The duckling
    c. The duckling's mother

17. Imagine that the duckling begins to drown in the river and cries for help. What would the loud duck probably do?
    a. Try to save the duckling's life
    b. Ignore the duckling's cries ✓
    c. Ask the duckling what he wanted

18. Why did the loud duck try to chase the duckling away?
    a. He wanted to protect the other ducks.
    b. He was mad at the duckling's mother.
    c. He didn't like ducks who were different. ✓

STOP—end of test—SCORE: _____

Recording Individual Results

(Use the following script to record individual results.)

1. Look at your Individual Skills Profile Chart.

2. You're going to record your test results for lesson 40. First look at the test to find out which items you got wrong. Then circle those items on the chart.

3. Now record your results. I'll help you if you have any questions. (Circulate among the students as they record their results.)

4. (After the students finish, say:) Now count the items you did not circle and write the total in the **Total** box near the bottom of the column. The total should be the same as your test score.

5. Now you'll fill in the other boxes for lesson 40. If you scored 0 to 14 points, write an **X** in the box marked **Retest.** If you scored 15 to 18 points, write your score in the box marked **FINAL SCORE.**

Remedial Exercises

Students who scored 0 to 14 points on the test should be given remedial help. After the regular reading period is over, assemble these students and present the following exercises. The students will need their original test papers.

EXERCISE 1   Vocabulary Review

1. Let's talk about the meanings of some words.

2. The first word is **bruise.** A **bruise** is a sore place on your body. It may be red, or it may be black and blue.
- Everybody, what do we call a black and blue mark? (Signal.) *A bruise.*

3. The next word is **straining.** When you make your body work as hard as it can, you're **straining** your body.
- Everybody, what's another way of saying **She was making her body work as hard as it could to lift the heavy rock?** (Signal.) *She was straining to lift the heavy rock.*

4. The next word is **thoroughbred.** A **thoroughbred** is a special breed of horse that is used for racing.
- Everybody, what do we call a special breed of horse that is used for racing? (Signal.) *A Thoroughbred.*

5. The next word is **gallop.** When horses **gallop,** they run almost as fast as they can.
- Everybody, what's another way of saying **The horses ran almost as fast as they could back to the barn because they were thirsty?** (Signal.) *The horses galloped back to the barn because they were thirsty.*

6. The next word is **dilapidated.** Something that is really broken down and in bad shape is **dilapidated.**
- Everybody, what do we call something that is really broken down and in bad shape? (Signal.) *Dilapidated.*

7. The next word is **nudge.** A **nudge** is a gentle push.
- Everybody, what do we call a gentle push? (Signal.) *A nudge.*

8. The next word is **pasture.** A **pasture** is a field for farm animals.
- Everybody, what's a pasture? (Signal.) *A field for farm animals.*

9. The last word is **relatives. Relatives** are people in your family.
- Everybody, what's another way of saying **We invited the people in our family to my birthday party?** (Signal.) *We invited our relatives to my birthday party.*

EXERCISE 2   General Review

1. You read a story that takes place in England. What is the name of that story? (Response: *A Horse to Remember.*)

2. What can Nellie do very well? (Idea: *Jump.*)

3. At the beginning of the story, why was Tara's father worried about Nellie's jumping? (Idea: *Nellie jumped over his fences.*)

4. How did Tara's father want to solve the problem with Nellie? (Idea: *By selling Nellie.*)

5. Why did Tara think of a different solution? (Idea: *She wanted to keep Nellie.*)

6. When a horse lands after a jump, which way can the horse's rider go? (Idea: *Forward.*)
So what should the rider do before the horse lands? (Ideas: *Lean backward; brace herself or himself.*)

7. Everybody, look at page 14 of your test and find the encyclopedia index.
Which book has an article about the Grand Canyon? (Response: *Book 17.*)

8. On what page does the article begin? (Response: *Page 342.*)

9. What article appears on page 461 of book 14? (Response: *Graphic Arts.*)

EXERCISE 3   Passage Reading

1. Everybody, look at the passage on page 15 of your test. You're going to read the passage aloud.

2. (Call on individual students to read several sentences each. Correct all decoding errors. When the students finish, present the following questions.)

3. How did the duckling get a small bruise on his neck? (Idea: *The loud duck bit him on the neck.*)

4. How did the big duck treat the duckling? (Ideas: *The big duck was mean to the duckling; the big duck bit the duckling.*)

5. How did the duckling feel after the big duck bit him? (Ideas: *The duckling was unhappy; he was in pain.*)

6. How will the duckling feel if he meets the big duck again? (Ideas: *Unhappy; afraid.*)

7. Where were some of the ducks swimming? (Idea: *In the river.*)

8. Which character was uncomfortable? (Response: *The duckling.*)

9. What do you think the duckling's mother would do if someone else made fun of the duckling? (Idea: *She would defend the duckling.*)

10. Why does the duckling's mother speak up for the duckling? (Idea: *She's his mother; she loves him.*)

Retesting the Students

After you've completed the remedial exercises, retest each student individually. To administer the retest, you will need the student's original test paper, a blank copy of the test, and a red pencil. Give the student the blank copy of the test. Say, "Look at page 14. You're going to take this test again. Read each item aloud and tell me the answer."

Use the student's original test paper to grade the retest. Use the red pencil to mark each correct answer with a **C** and each incorrect answer with an **X.** Then count one point for each correct answer and write the new score at the bottom of the page. Finally, revise the Individual Skills Profile Chart by drawing an **X** over any items the student missed on the retest.

Fluency: Rate/Accuracy

Administer the fluency checkout for lesson 40. The passage begins on page 56. For further instructions, see page 52.

Tested Skills

The following list shows the test items and the skills they test.
- using vocabulary words in context (items 1–3)
- using context to predict word meaning (items 4–6)
- recalling details and events (item 7)
- evaluating problems and solutions (item 8)
- drawing conclusions (item 9)
- interpreting a character's motives (item 10)
- interpreting indexes and headings (items 11 and 12)
- identifying literal cause and effect (item 13)
- predicting narrative outcomes (item 14)
- answering literal questions about a text (item 15)
- distinguishing characters by trait (item 16)
- predicting a character's actions (item 17)
- inferring a character's point of view (item 18)

LESSON 50

Administering the Test

The Lesson 50 Mastery Test should be administered after the students complete all work on lesson 50 and before they begin work on lesson 51. Each student will need a pencil and a copy of the *Curriculum-Based Assessment and Fluency Student Book.* Use the following script.

1. (Have the students clear their desks. Make sure each student has a pencil.)

2. Now you're going to take another test on what you've learned. Don't begin until I tell you.

3. Write your name on the name line.

4. Now you're ready to begin the test. Answer all the items on both pages. There is no time limit. When you've finished, turn your test facedown and look up at me. Begin the test now. (If you are including the writing item as part of the testing session, tell students they can begin the writing item after they finish the mastery test.)

Grading the Test

You can grade the tests yourself, or you can have the students grade their own tests. If you want the students to grade their own tests, use the following script.

1. Now we're going to grade the test. I'll read the correct answer for each item. If the answer is correct, mark it with a **C.** If the answer is wrong, mark it with an **X.**

2. (Read the correct answers from the answer key in the next column.)

3. Now count the number of **correct** answers and enter the score at the end of the test.

Answer Key

LESSON 50

Name _____

For items 1–6, circle the letter of the answer that means the same thing as the underlined part.

1. I gave my cousin a warm <u>hug</u> at the reunion.
   - (a.) embrace
   - b. prey
   - c. crest

2. The fire fighter <u>came down</u> the ladder.
   - a. exchanged
   - (b.) descended
   - c. tolerated

3. Dogs have a <u>very good</u> sense of smell.
   - (a.) keen
   - b. treacherous
   - c. miserable

4. Ricardo had great <u>affection</u> for his children.
   - a. hatred
   - (b.) fondness
   - c. indifference

5. I am going to <u>bargain</u> with the automobile salesperson.
   - a. fight
   - b. argue
   - (c.) deal

6. Did you <u>witness</u> the accident yesterday?
   - a. cause
   - b. photograph
   - (c.) see

For items 7–18, circle the letter of the correct answer.

7. What is the main idea of the picture below?

   Maria

   - a. Maria has long hair.
   - (b.) Maria is tying her shoe.
   - c. Maria is wearing pants.

8. Which one of the following is fiction?
   - (a.) A short story about a talking bear
   - b. A newspaper article about a basketball game
   - c. An encyclopedia entry about farming

9. How was the cat different from the other animals?
   - a. He lived with people.
   - b. He was domesticated.
   - (c.) He walked by himself.

10. Which city was filled with gold miners?
    - (a.) Dawson
    - b. London
    - c. Liverpool

11. What are the great ice floes between mountains called?
    - (a.) glaciers
    - b. galaxies
    - c. tornadoes

12. Which animal saved his master's life?
    - a. First Friend
    - (b.) Buck
    - c. Giver of Good Food

Read the passage below. Then answer items 13–18.

The crowd fell silent. Everybody knew that Buck was a magnificent animal; but the thousand pounds of flour was more than any dog could pull.

Thornton knelt by Buck's side. He took the dog's head in his two hands and rested his cheek on Buck's cheek. He did not playfully shake him or murmur softly. But he whispered something in the dog's ear. Buck whined eagerly.

The crowd was watching curiously. The affair was growing mysterious. It seemed like a magic trick. As Thornton got to his feet, Buck seized Thornton's hand between his jaws, pressing it with his teeth and releasing slowly. It was Buck's answer.

Thornton stepped back. "Now, Buck," he said. Buck pulled his harness tight, then let it slacken a bit.

"Gee!" Thornton's voice rang out, sharp in the tense silence.

Buck followed the command. He swung to the right, ending the movement in a lunge that jerked the harness and stopped his one hundred and fifty pounds. The load quivered, and a crisp crackling rose from under the runners.

"Haw!" Thornton commanded.

Buck made the same move, this time to the left. The crackling turned into a snapping. The sled turned slightly, and the runners slipped and grated several inches to the side. The sled was broken out. Men were holding their breath.

"Now, MUSH ON!"

13. What made the crackling noise when the sled moved?
    - (a.) The runners breaking out of the snow
    - b. The bags of flour rubbing against each other
    - c. Buck's feet digging into the snow

14. What does the command "Haw" mean?
    - (a.) Move to the left.
    - b. Move to the right.
    - c. Move straight ahead.

15. What will Buck probably do next?
    - a. Push the sled backwards
    - b. Lie down and rest
    - (c.) Pull the sled straight ahead

16. How did Buck answer Thornton after Thornton whispered in Buck's ear?
    - a. By barking loudly
    - b. By wagging his tail
    - (c.) By biting Thornton's hand

17. How did Buck feel about Thornton?
    - a. He was afraid of Thornton.
    - b. He disliked Thornton.
    - (c.) He loved Thornton.

18. Why did Thornton kneel at Buck's side?
    - a. He wanted to warm Buck's legs.
    - (b.) He wanted to encourage Buck.
    - c. He wanted to feed Buck.

STOP—end of test—SCORE: _____

Recording Individual Results

(Use the following script to record individual results.)

1. Look at your Individual Skills Profile Chart.

2. You're going to record your test results for lesson 50. First look at the test to find out which items you got wrong. Then circle those items on the chart.

3. Now record your results. I'll help you if you have any questions. (Circulate among the students as they record their results.)

4. (After the students finish, say:) Now count the items you did not circle and write the total in the **Total** box near the bottom of the column. The total should be the same as your test score.

5. Now you'll fill in the other boxes for lesson 50. If you scored 0 to 14 points, write an **X** in the box marked **Retest.** If you scored 15 to 18 points, write your score in the box marked **FINAL SCORE.**

Remedial Exercises

Students who scored 0 to 14 points on the test should be given remedial help. After the regular reading period is over, assemble these students and present the following exercises. The students will need their original test papers.

EXERCISE 1   Vocabulary Review

1. Let's talk about the meanings of some words.

2. The first word is **embrace.** An **embrace** is a hug.
- Everybody, what's another way of saying **She gave him a hug?** (Signal.) *She gave him an embrace.*

3. The next word is **treacherous. Treacherous** means "very dangerous."
- Everybody, what's another way of saying **The trail was very dangerous?** (Signal.) *The trail was treacherous.*

4. The next word is **affection. Affection** is another word for **fondness.**

- Everybody, what's another way of saying **The cat was used to a lot of fondness?** (Signal.) *The cat was used to a lot of affection.*

5. The next word is **descend.** When something **descends,** it comes down.
- Everybody, what's another way of saying **The dog came down the staircase?** (Signal.) *The dog descended the staircase.*

6. The next word is **keen.** If your hearing is very good, you have **keen** hearing.
- Everybody, what's another way of saying **He has very good hearing?** (Signal.) *He has keen hearing.*

7. The next word is **lean.** Someone who has very little fat is **lean.**
- Everybody, what's another way of saying **Long-distance runners have very little fat?** (Signal.) *Long-distance runners are lean.*

8. The next word is **witness.** When you **witness** an event, you see that event happening.
- Everybody, what's another way of saying **He saw the tree falling?** (Signal.) *He witnessed the tree falling.*

9. The last word is **lunge.** When people **lunge,** they charge forward suddenly.
- Everybody, what's another way of saying **The children charged forward suddenly for the candy on the table?** (Signal.) *The children lunged for the candy on the table.*

EXERCISE 2   General Review

1. Was the story "The Cat That Walked by Himself" factual or fictional? (**Response:** *Fictional.*)

2. How do you know it was fictional? (Idea: *It told about things that never happened.*)

3. Was the article "The Domestication of Animals" factual or fictional? (**Response:** *Factual.*)

4. How do you know it was factual? (Idea: *It told about events that really happened.*)

5. What was the name of the town along the Yukon River? (**Response:** *Dawson.*)

6. Why did many people go to that town? (Idea: *To look for gold*.)

7. What position did Buck have in the dog sled team? (Idea: *He was the lead dog.*)

8. Which story takes place in the Yukon Valley? (Response: *"Buck."*)

EXERCISE 3   Passage Reading

1. Everybody, look at the passage on page 18 of your test. You're going to read the passage aloud.

2. (Call on individual students to read several sentences each. Correct all decoding errors. When the students finish, present the following questions.)

3. At the beginning of the passage, what was wrong with the runners of the sled? (Idea: *They were frozen in the snow.*)

4. How could Thornton tell that the runners of the sled had broken free of the snow? (Idea: *He heard a crackling noise; the sled began to move.*)

5. In which direction did Buck move when Thornton said "Gee"? (Response: *Right.*)

6. So what does the command "Gee" mean? (Idea: *Move to the right.*)

7. What does the command "Mush on" mean? (Idea: *Move forward.*)

8. So what will Buck do when he hears that command? (Idea: *Move forward.*)

9. What did Buck bite? (Idea: *Thornton's hand.*)

10. Why do you think Buck worked so hard for Thornton? (Ideas: *Buck loved Thornton; Thornton was Buck's master.*)

11. Why do you think Thornton whispered in Buck's ear? (Ideas: *To give Buck encouragement; to tell Buck he was a good dog.*)

Retesting the Students

After you've completed the remedial exercises, retest each student individually. To administer the retest, you will need the student's original test paper, a blank copy of the test, and a red pencil. Give the student the blank copy of the test. Say, "Look at page 17. You're going to take this test again. Read each item aloud and tell me the answer."

Use the student's original test paper to grade the retest. Use the red pencil to mark each correct answer with a **C** and each incorrect answer with an **X**. Then count one point for each correct answer and write the new score at the bottom of the page. Finally, revise the Individual Skills Profile Chart by drawing an **X** over any items the student missed on the retest.

Fluency: Rate/Accuracy

Administer the fluency checkout for lesson 50. The passage begins on page 57. For further instructions, see page 52.

Tested Skills

The following list shows the test items and the skills they test.
- using vocabulary words in context (items 1–3)
- using context to predict word meaning (items 4–6)
- inferring the main idea (item 7)
- distinguishing between fact and fiction (item 8)
- making comparisons (item 9)
- distinguishing settings by features (item 10)
- recalling details and events (item 11)
- distinguishing characters by trait (item 12)
- inferring causes and effects (item 13)
- inferring story details and events (item 14)
- predicting narrative outcomes (item 15)
- answering literal questions about a text (item 16)
- interpreting a character's feelings (item 17)
- interpreting a character's motives (item 18)

LESSON 60

Administering the Test

The Lesson 60 Mastery Test should be administered after the students complete all work on lesson 60 and before they begin work on lesson 61. Each student will need a pencil and a copy of the *Curriculum-Based Assessment and Fluency Student Book.* Use the following script.

1. (Have the students clear their desks. Make sure each student has a pencil.)

2. Now you're going to take another test on what you've learned. This test will be longer than the others you've taken because it has questions about the last thirty lessons. Don't begin until I tell you.

3. Write your name on the name line.

4. Now you're ready to begin the test. Answer all the items on each page. There is no time limit. When you've finished, turn your test facedown and look up at me. Begin the test now. (If you are including the writing item as part of the testing session, tell students they can begin the writing item after they finish the mastery test.)

Grading the Test

You can grade the tests yourself, or you can have the students grade their own tests. If you want the students to grade their own tests, use the following script.

1. Now we're going to grade the test. I'll read the correct answer for each item. If the answer is correct, mark it with a **C.** If the answer is wrong, mark it with an **X.**

2. (Read the correct answers from the answer key on this page and the following.)

3. Now count the number of **correct** answers and enter the score at the end of the test.

Answer Key

Lesson 60

1.	c	28.	a
2.	a	29.	a
3.	b	30.	a
4.	a	31.	c
5.	b	32.	b
6.	a	33.	a
7.	c	34.	b
8.	a	35.	a
9.	b	36.	c
10.	a	37.	b
11.	c	38.	c
12.	a	39.	a
13.	b	40.	c
14.	a	41.	a
15.	c	42.	c
16.	b	43.	a
17.	b	44.	c
18.	a	45.	b
19.	b	46.	a
20.	b	47.	c
21.	a	48.	b
22.	c	49.	c
23.	a	50.	a
24.	c	51.	a
25.	a	52.	b
26.	b	53.	c
27.	a		

Recording Individual Results

(Use the following script to record individual results.)

1. Look at your Individual Skills Profile Chart.

2. You're going to record your test results for lesson 60. First look at the test to find out which items you got wrong. Then circle those items on the chart.

3. Now record your results. I'll help you if you have any questions. (Circulate among the students as they record their results.)

4. (After the students finish, say:) Now count the items you did not circle and write the total in the **Total** box near the bottom of the column. The total should be the same as your test score.

5. Now you'll fill in the other boxes for lesson 60. If you scored 0 to 43 points, write an **X** in the box marked **Retest.** If you scored 44 to 53 points, write your score in the box marked **FINAL SCORE.**

Remedial Exercises

Students who scored 0 to 43 points on the test should be given remedial help. After the regular reading period is over, assemble these students and present the following exercises. The students will need their original test papers.

EXERCISE 1	Vocabulary Review

1. Let's talk about the meanings of some words.

2. The first word is **develops. Develops** is another word for **grows.**
- Everybody, what's another way of saying **His tennis skill is growing?** (Signal.) *His tennis skill is developing.*

3. The next word is **spectators.** People who watch an event are **spectators.**
- Everybody, what's another way of saying **The people watching the event cheered for their team?** (Signal.) *The spectators cheered for their team.*

4. The next word is **pounce. Pounce** is another word for **jump.**
- Everybody, what's another way of saying **The tiger jumped on its prey?** (Signal.) *The tiger pounced on its prey.*

5. The next word is **accept.** When you **accept** a gift, you take it.
- Everybody, what's another way of saying **Please take my apology?** (Signal.) *Please accept my apology.*

6. The next word is **plentiful. Plentiful** means "in good supply."
- Everybody, what's another way of saying **Oranges are in good supply this year?** (Signal.) *Oranges are plentiful this year.*

7. The next word is **identify.** When you **identify** something, you tell what it is.
- Everybody, what's another way of saying **Can you tell what kind of flower this is?** (Signal.) *Can you identify this flower?*

8. The next word is **reluctant.** When you don't want to do something very much, you are **reluctant** to do it.
- Everybody, what's another way of saying **She didn't want to go to the beach very much?** (Signal.) *She was reluctant to go to the beach.*

9. The next word is **quail.** A **quail** is a bird about the size of a pigeon.
- Everybody, what's another way of saying **People in the Southeast hunt for birds about the size of pigeons?** (Signal.) *People in the Southeast hunt for quails.*

10. The next word is **sprawling.** If something is **spread out,** it is sprawling.
- Everybody, what's another way of saying **This certainly is a spread-out city?** (Signal.) *This certainly is a sprawling city.*

11. The next word is **intently.** When you are concentrating on listening, you are listening **intently.**
- Everybody, what's another way of saying **She is concentrating on studying?** (Signal.) *She is studying intently.*

12. The last word is **species. Species** is another word for type.

- Everybody, what's another way of saying **Dogs are an interesting type of animal?** (Signal.) *Dogs are an interesting species of animal.*

EXERCISE 2   General Review

1. What did the ugly duckling hatch from? (Response: *An egg.*)

2. What did the ugly duckling grow into? (Idea: *A beautiful swan.*)

3. Did the duckling fly **before** or **after** the winter? (Response: *After.*)

4. What main thing does the story "A Horse to Remember" tell about? (Idea: *A horse named Nellie.*)

5. What could Nellie do well? (Idea: *Jump.*)

6. What direction is always on the right side of a map? (Response: *East.*)

7. Listen to the following passage. **Some houses are made of brick. Some churches are made of brick. Some schools are made of brick.**

- What are the three things that are named? (Idea: *Houses, churches, schools.*)
- What's a class name for houses, churches, and schools? (Response: *Buildings.*)
- What are some buildings made of? (Response: *Brick.*)
- Say the whole main idea. (Idea: *Some buildings are made of brick.*)

8. What was the first animal to become domesticated? (Idea: *The dog.*)

9. What were dogs first used for? (Idea: *Hunting.*)

10. What are some animals that give food? (Ideas: *Sheep, cattle, chickens.*)

11. What is the journey like from Juneau to Dawson? (Idea: *Long and dangerous.*)

12. Why are things expensive in Skagway? (Idea: *Everything has to be brought in.*)

13. Was the article "Amazing Animal Journeys" fact or fiction? (Response: *Fact.*)

- How do you know it was fact? (Idea: *It told about real things and events.*)

14. What kind of animal is the tanager? (Idea: *A bird.*)

15. What is the name for a bird's process of shedding old feathers and growing new ones? (Idea: *Molting.*)

16. How do scientists track animals as they travel? (Idea: *They tag the animals.*)

17. How do salmon get back to their homes? (Idea: *They swim upstream.*)

18. Where is a woodchuck's home? (Idea: *In an underground den.*)

19. What does a caterpillar change into? (Idea: *A butterfly.*)

20. Which story takes place in North Carolina? (Response: *Adventure on the Rocky Ridge.*)

21. How did Martha get Mr. Owl's scent? (Idea: *From his glove.*)

22. What do the African elephant, the blue whale, and the bald eagle have in common? (Idea: *They are in danger of extinction.*)

23. Why did sailors kill Galápagos tortoises? (Idea: *For food.*)

24. Pretend you are in Canada. What direction would you go to get to Alaska? (Response: *West.*)

25. Pretend you are in California. What direction would you go to get to Alaska? (Response: *North.*)

EXERCISE 3   Passage Reading

Passage 1

1. Everybody, look at the passage on page 21 of your test. You're going to read the passage aloud.

2. (Call on individual students to read several sentences each. Correct all decoding errors. When the students finish, present the following questions.)

3. At the beginning of the passage, what did Tara's father tell her? (Idea: *That the Briggs family might have to get rid of Nellie.*)

4. How did Tara feel about that? (Idea: *Discouraged.*)

5. What was wrong with all the ideas that Tara thought of for keeping Nellie? (Idea: *The ideas cost money.*)

6. What kept popping into Tara's mind? (Idea: *The instant she first saw Nellie leaping the fence.*)

7. What did Tara think Nellie probably was? (Idea: *The greatest jumping horse in the world.*)

8. Why did Tara get up early? (Idea: *To find out about jumping horses.*)

Passage 2

1. Everybody, look at the passage on page 22 of your test. You're going to read the passage aloud.

2. (Call on individual students to read several sentences each. Correct all decoding errors. When the students finish, present the following questions.)

3. At the beginning of the passage, what did the man say to try to get the dogs to get up? (Idea: *"Mush on."*)

4. What was Thornton doing as he listened to the man? (Idea: *Whittling.*)

5. What did Thornton think was a bad idea? (Idea: *To get between a fool and his foolish ideas.*)

6. How many dogs got up? (Response: *Four.*)

7. What did Buck do when he was whipped? (Idea: *He lay quietly.*)

8. Why did Buck refuse to move? (Ideas: *He had a feeling of disaster; he sensed death.*)

Passage 3

1. Everybody, look at the passage on page 24 of your test. You're going to read the passage aloud.

2. (Call on individual students to read several sentences each. Correct all decoding errors. When the students finish, present the following questions.)

3. What did all the dogs that Mr. Owl raised have? (Idea: *A powerful sense of smell.*)

4. What didn't Mr. Owl know at the time? (Ideas: *That Martha's nose was more sensitive than the nose of any other dog he had ever raised; that Martha's nose was better than the nose of any other dog in North Carolina.*)

5. What could Martha recognize even with her eyes closed? (Idea: *Julie's smell.*)

6. What did Julie's smell mean to Martha? (Ideas: *Warm milk, soft petting, a nice blanket to keep her warm.*)

7. Where did Mr. Owl put the puppies for the hunting-dog test? (Idea: *In the box.*)

8. Where did Mr. Owl put the mother dog for the test? (Idea: *Outside the box.*)

9. What did the best puppies do? (Idea: *They banged their heads to get to their mother.*)

Retesting the Students

After you've completed the remedial exercises, retest each student individually. To administer the retest, you will need the student's original test paper, a blank copy of the test, and a red pencil. Give the student the blank copy of the test. Say, "Look at page 20. You're going to take this test again. Read each item aloud and tell me the answer."

Use the student's original test paper to grade the retest. Use the red pencil to mark each correct answer with a **C** and each incorrect answer with an **X.** Then count one point for each correct answer and write the new score at the bottom of the page. Finally, revise the Individual Skills Profile Chart by drawing an **X** over any items the student missed on the retest.

Fluency: Rate/Accuracy

Administer the fluency checkout for lesson 60. The passage begins on page 58. For further instructions, see page 52.

Tested Skills

The following list shows the test items and the skills they test.

- using vocabulary words in context (items 1–6)
- using context to predict word meaning (items 7–12)
- making comparisons (items 13 and 42)
- inferring cause and effect (items 14 and 35)
- inferring story details and events (items 15 and 41)
- predicting a character's actions (items 16 and 53)
- interpreting indexes and headings (items 17 and 18)
- evaluating problems and solutions (items 19 and 50)
- drawing conclusions (items 20 and 46)
- identifying literal cause and effect (items 21 and 26)
- answering literal questions about a text (items 22 and 34)
- inferring a character's point of view (item 23)
- predicting narrative outcomes (items 24 and 45)
- distinguishing characters by traits (items 25, 39, and 52)
- inferring the main idea (items 27, 48, and 49)
- recalling details and events (items 28 and 40)
- interpreting maps (items 29 and 30)
- distinguishing settings by features (item 31)
- interpreting a character's feelings (items 32 and 51)
- interpreting a character's motives (items 33 and 37)
- sequencing narrative events (items 36 and 44)
- relating titles to story content (items 38 and 43)
- distinguishing between fact and fiction (item 47)

LESSON 70

Administering the Test

The Lesson 70 Mastery Test should be administered after the students complete all work on lesson 70 and before they begin work on lesson 71. Each student will need a pencil and a copy of the *Curriculum-Based Assessment and Fluency Student Book.* Use the following script.

1. (Have the students clear their desks. Make sure each student has a pencil.)

2. Now you're going to take another test on what you've learned. Don't begin until I tell you.

3. Write your name on the name line.

4. Now you're ready to begin the test. Answer all the items on each page. There is no time limit. When you've finished, turn your test facedown and look up at me. Begin the test now. (If you are including the writing item as part of the testing session, tell students they can begin the writing item after they finish the mastery test.)

Grading the Test

You can grade the tests yourself, or you can have the students grade their own tests. If you want the students to grade their own tests, use the following script.

1. Now we're going to grade the test. I'll read the correct answer for each item. If the answer is correct, mark it with a **C.** If the answer is wrong, mark it with an **X.**

2. (Read the correct answers from the answer key on this page and the following.)

3. Now count the number of **correct** answers and enter the score at the end of the test.

Answer Key

Lesson 70

1. b
2. a
3. c
4. b
5. b
6. c
7. b
8. a
9. a
10. b
11. c
12. c
13. b
14. a
15. a
16. a
17. c
18. c
19. b
20. a
21. b
22. b

Recording Individual Results

(Use the following script to record individual results.)

1. Look at your Individual Skills Profile Chart.

2. You're going to record your test results for lesson 70. First look at the test to find out which items you got wrong. Then circle those items on the chart.

3. Now record your results. I'll help you if you have any questions. (Circulate among the students as they record their results.)

4. (After the students finish, say:) Now count the items you did not circle and write the total in the **Total** box near the bottom of the column. The total should be the same as your test score.

5. Now you'll fill in the other boxes for lesson 70. If you scored 0 to 17 points, write an **X** in the box marked **Retest.** If you scored 18 to 22 points, write your score in the box marked **FINAL SCORE.**

Remedial Exercises

Students who scored 0 to 17 points on the test should be given remedial help. After the regular reading period is over, assemble these students and present the following exercises. The students will need their original test papers.

EXERCISE 1   Vocabulary Review

1. Let's talk about the meanings of some words.

2. The first word is **glossy.** Something that is very smooth and shiny is **glossy.**
- Everybody, what do we call hair that is very smooth and shiny? (Signal.) *Glossy hair.*

3. The next word is **decent.** Another word for **good** is **decent.**
- Everybody, what's another way of saying **She was a good person?** (Signal.) *She was a decent person.*

4. The next word is **greedy.** When you are **greedy** you are not satisfied with what you have.
- Everybody, what's another way of saying **The rich man was not satisfied with what he had?** (Signal.) *The rich man was greedy.*

5. The next word is **deserve.** When you **deserve** something, you are worthy of that thing.

- Everybody, what's another way of saying **You are worthy of an A on your test?** (Signal.) *You deserve an A on your test.*

6. The next word is **narrator.** A **narrator** is a person who tells a story.
- Everybody, what do we call a person who tells a story? (Signal.) *A narrator.*

7. The next word is **linen. Linen** is an expensive cloth that some sheets and dresses are made of.
- Everybody, what's an expensive cloth that some sheets and dresses are made of? (Signal.) *Linen.*

8. The next word is **oppose.** When you are against an idea, you **oppose** that idea.
- Everybody, what's another way of saying **Nobody was against the idea?** (Signal.) *Nobody opposed the idea.*

9. The next word is **calculate. Calculate** means "figure out."
- Everybody, what's another way of saying **The waiter figured out the bill?** (Signal.) *The waiter calculated the bill.*

10. The next word is **promoted.** When you are **promoted,** you get a more important job.
- Everybody, what happens to you when you get a more important job? (Signal.) *You are promoted.*

11. The next word is **appetite.** Your **appetite** is your desire for food.
- Everybody, what do we call your desire for food? (Signal.) *Your appetite.*

12. The next word is **plant. Plant** is another word for **factory.**
- Everybody, what's another way of saying **a tire factory?** (Signal.) *A tire plant.*

13. The last word is **inhale.** When you breathe in, you **inhale.**
- Everybody, what's another way of saying **They breathed in the morning air?** (Signal.) *They inhaled the morning air.*

EXERCISE 2   General Review

1. What sport did Jackie Robinson play? (Response: *Baseball.*)

2. What kind of animal did Robinson's neighbor

Carl Anderson say Robinson was behaving like? (Response: *A sheep.*)

3. How was Robinson like a sheep? (Idea: *Sheep are animals that all follow one sheep without thinking.*)

4. Before Jackie Robinson put on a Dodger uniform, what did he have to promise Branch Rickey he wouldn't do? (Ideas: *Fight; argue; cause any kind of trouble.*)

5. Everybody, look at the time line on page 27 of your test.
• In which year did Robinson first play for the Dodgers? (Response: *1947.*)
• What did Robinson do in 1941? (Idea: *He left UCLA.*)

6. Now look at the map on page 27.
• What state does the map show? (Response: *California.*)
• What do the dots show? (Response: *Cities.*)
• What do the triangles show? (Response: *Mountains.*)
• Which mountain is the farthest north? (Response: *M.*)

EXERCISE 3   Passage Reading

1. Everybody, look at the passage on page 27 of your test. You're going to read the passage aloud.

2. (Call on individual students to read several sentences each. Correct all decoding errors. When the students finish, present the following questions.)

3. What happened to all the things Midas touched? (Idea: *They turned into gold.*)

4. Name some things that Midas turned into gold. (Ideas: *His breakfast, Marygold.*)

5. Why was Midas hungry? (Idea: *He could not eat anything.*)

6. What would Midas have to do in order to eat? (Idea: *Get rid of the Golden Touch.*)

7. What did Midas think was worth a thousand times the Golden Touch? (Idea: *His daughter's love.*)

8. What color would a piece of paper become if Midas touched it? (Ideas: *Yellow, gold.*)

9. Which character was able to eat breakfast? (Response: *Marygold.*)
• So how did Midas feel when he saw Marygold eating? (Idea: *Envious.*)

Retesting the Students

After you have completed the remedial exercises, retest each student individually. To administer the retest, you will need the student's original test paper, a blank copy of the test, and a red pencil. Give the student the blank copy of the test. Say, "Look at page 26. You're going to take this test again. Read each item aloud and tell me the answer."

Use the student's original test paper to grade the retest. Use the red pencil to mark each correct answer with a **C** and each incorrect answer with an **X**. Then count one point for each correct answer and write the new score at the bottom of the page. Finally, revise the Individual Skills Profile Chart by drawing an **X** over any items the student missed on the retest.

Fluency: Rate/Accuracy

Administer the fluency checkout for lesson 70. The passage begins on page 59. For further instructions, see page 52.

Tested Skills

The following list shows the test items and the skills they test.
• using vocabulary words in context (items 1–4)
• using context to predict word meaning (items 5–8)
• recalling details and events (item 9)
• making comparisons (item 10)
• distinguishing characters by traits (item 11)
• inferring the main idea (item 12)
• interpreting time lines (items 13 and 14)
• interpreting maps (items 15 and 16)
• inferring story details and events (item 17)
• evaluating problems and solutions (item 18)
• predicting a character's actions (item 19)
• inferring a character's point of view (item 20)
• identifying literal cause and effect (item 21)
• interpreting a character's feelings (item 22)

LESSON 80

Administering the Test

The Lesson 80 Mastery Test should be administered after the students complete all work on lesson 80 and before they begin work on lesson 81. Each student will need a pencil and a copy of the *Curriculum-Based Assessment and Fluency Student Book*. Use the following script.

1. (Have the students clear their desks. Make sure each student has a pencil.)

2. Now you're going to take another test on what you've learned. Don't begin until I tell you.

3. Write your name on the name line.

4. Now you're ready to begin the test. Answer all the items on each page. There is no time limit. When you've finished, turn your test facedown and look up at me. Begin the test now. (If you are including the writing item as part of the testing session, tell students they can begin the writing item after they finish the mastery test.)

Grading the Test

You can grade the tests yourself, or you can have the students grade their own tests. If you want the students to grade their own tests, use the following script.

1. Now we're going to grade the test. I'll read the correct answer for each item. If the answer is correct, mark it with a **C.** If the answer is wrong, mark it with an **X.**

2. (Read the correct answers from the answer key in the next column.)

3. Now count the number of **correct** answers and enter the score at the end of the test.

Answer Key

LESSON 80

Name _____

For items 1–8, circle the letter of the answer that means the same thing as the underlined part.

1. My grandmother is a smart investor.
   a. shrewd ✓
   b. fertile
   c. spacious

2. She expressed great sorrow at hearing the sad news.
   a. poverty
   b. grief ✓
   c. fragrance

3. There are a lot of supplies for your projects.
   a. abundant ✓
   b. nimble
   c. witty

4. We got a new fancy light with many ornaments for the entryway.
   a. chariot
   b. chandelier ✓
   c. portrait

5. The inhabitants of that town are quite friendly.
   a. buildings in
   b. people who live in ✓
   c. victims of

6. There is no trace of anyone in the cafeteria today.
   a. picture of
   b. mystery about
   c. clue of ✓

7. Do you believe in spells?
   a. magic charms ✓
   b. biographies
   c. myths

8. I am dreading the test because I didn't study for it.
   a. excited about
   b. not looking forward to ✓
   b. mailing in

For items 9–23, circle the letter of the correct answer.

9. What is the tallest mountain in Greece?
   a. Mount Zeus
   b. Mount Golden
   c. Mount Olympus ✓

10. Which deity played jokes on the other deities?
    a. Hermes ✓
    b. Ares
    c. Hades

11. What did Baucis and Philemon do first?
    a. They saw a new lake.
    b. They saw two strangers approaching. ✓
    c. They turned into trees.

12. Why were Baucis and Philemon kind to strangers?
    a. To make up for the rudeness of their neighbors ✓
    b. So that everyone would like them
    c. So that people would pay them

13. What is one lesson from "The Miraculous Pitcher"?
    a. Be careful with strangers.
    b. Do not talk to strangers.
    c. Be kind to strangers. ✓

14. How is a folktale different from a myth?
    a. A folktale often has beautiful girls, while a myth has only ugly girls.
    b. A folktale often has witches and wizards, while a myth usually has gods and goddesses. ✓
    c. A folktale often has evil people, while a myth has only good people.

15. Why did Beauty agree to go to the Beast with her father?
    a. She was curious about the Beast.
    b. She wanted to help her father keep his promise. ✓
    c. She wanted to get away from her brothers and sisters.

16. Pretend you are reading an encyclopedia article about Greece. Which heading would you look under to find facts about Mount Olympus?
    a. Farming in Greece
    b. The Olympic Games
    c. Mountains in Greece ✓

17. Which one of the following is fiction?
    a. A short story about a girl detective ✓
    b. A history of pioneer life
    c. An encyclopedia entry about the Stone Age

Read the passage below. Then answer items 18–23.

Beauty and her father had hardly finished their meal when they heard the Beast approaching. Beauty clung to her father in terror, which became all the greater when she saw how frightened he was. But when the Beast appeared, Beauty made a great effort to hide her terror. She bowed to him respectfully and thanked him for his hospitality. Her behavior seemed to please the Beast. After looking at her, he said, in a tone that might have struck terror in the boldest heart, "Good evening, sir. Good evening, Beauty."

The merchant was too terrified to reply, but Beauty answered sweetly, "Good evening, Beast."

"Have you come willingly?" asked the Beast. "Will you be content to stay here when your father goes away?"

Beauty answered bravely that she was quite prepared to stay.

"I am pleased with you," said the Beast. "You seem to have come of your own choice, so you may stay. As for you, sir," he added, turning to the merchant, "at sunrise tomorrow you will leave. When the bell rings, get up and eat your breakfast. You will find the same horse waiting to take you home. But remember that you must never expect to see my palace again."

18. What is the main idea of the first paragraph?
    a. Beauty was polite in spite of being frightened. ✓
    b. Beauty's father was more frightened than Beauty was.
    c. Beauty thanked the Beast for his hospitality.

19. What is the main idea of the last paragraph?
    a. The merchant will eat when the bell rings.
    b. Beauty could stay, but the merchant had to leave. ✓
    c. Beauty came of her own choice.

20. What is the most likely reason the Beast's voice struck terror in people's hearts?
    a. It was calm and quiet.
    b. It was high pitched and squeaky.
    c. It was deep and booming. ✓

21. Why might the Beast be pleased with Beauty's behavior?
    a. He could see that she had good manners.
    b. He could tell that she liked the meal.
    c. He wanted friends. ✓

22. Why do you think the title of the story is "Beauty and the Beast"?
    a. Both characters' names start with B.
    b. The characters are opposites in their looks.
    c. The story is about the characters' friendship. ✓

23. What will Beauty probably do after her father leaves?
    a. She will run away and catch up with her father.
    b. She will be kind to the Beast. ✓
    c. She will steal from the Beast.

STOP—end of test—SCORE: _____

Recording Individual Results

(Use the following script to record individual results.)

1. Look at your Individual Skills Profile Chart.

2. You're going to record your test results for lesson 80. First look at the test to find out which items you got wrong. Then circle those items on the chart.

3. Now record your results. I'll help you if you have any questions. (Circulate among the students as they record their results.)

4. (After the students finish, say:) Now count the items you did not circle and write the total in the **Total** box near the bottom of the column. The total should be the same as your test score.

5. Now you'll fill in the other boxes for lesson 80. If you scored 0 to 18 points, write an **X** in the box marked **Retest.** If you scored 19 to 23 points, write your score in the box marked **FINAL SCORE.**

Remedial Exercises

Students who scored 0 to 18 points on the test should be given remedial help. After the regular reading period is over, assemble these students and present the following exercises. The students will need their original test papers.

EXERCISE 1   Vocabulary Review

1. Let's talk about the meaning of some words.

2. The first word is **deity.** A **deity** is a god or goddess.
- Everybody, what's another way of saying **We read a myth about a Greek god?** (Signal.) *We read a myth about a Greek deity.*

3. The next word is **shrewed. Shrewd** is another word for smart.
- Everybody, what's another way of saying **The chess player made smart moves?** (Signal.) *The chess player made shrewd moves.*

4. The next word is **dread.** When you **dread** something, you don't look forward to it.

- Everybody, what's another way of saying **She didn't look forward to skating?** (Signal.) *She dreaded skating.*

5. The next word is **grief. Grief** means "great sorrow."
- Everybody, what's another way of saying **He felt great sorrow?** (Signal.) *He felt grief.*

6. The next word is **toil.** When you **toil,** you work hard.
- Everybody, what's another way of saying **My brother works hard at his lawn-mowing job?** (Signal.) *My brother toils at his lawn-mowing job.*

7. The next word is **sympathy.** When you show **sympathy** toward somebody, you share that person's feelings.
- Everybody, what's another way of saying **It is a kindness to share a person's feelings?** (Signal.) *It is a kindness to show sympathy.*

8. The next word is **inhabitant.** Someone who lives in a place is an **inhabitant** of that place.
- Everybody, what's another way of saying **The people who live in that town are rude?** (Signal.) *The inhabitants of that town are rude.*

9. The next word is **spacious.** When something has a lot of space in it, it is **spacious.**
- Everybody, what's another way of saying **The meeting hall has a lot of space in it?** (Signal.) *The meeting hall is spacious.*

10. The next word is **victim.** Somebody who is harmed is a **victim.**
- Everybody, what's another way of saying **Ben was harmed in the accident?** (Signal.) *Ben was a victim in the accident.*

11. The next word is **terrify. Terrify** means "greatly frighten."
- Everybody, what's another way of saying **A shark would greatly frighten me?** (Signal.) *A shark would terrify me.*

12. The next word is **refuse.** When you **refuse** an offer, you say no to the offer.
- Everybody, what's another way of saying **We said no to his offer to cook us dinner?** (Signal.) *We refused his offer to cook us dinner.*

13. The last word is **abundant.** If there is a lot of something, that thing is **abundant.**

- Everybody, what's another way of saying **There was a lot of rain this year?** (Signal.) *There was abundant rain this year.*

EXERCISE 2   General Review

1. Which two gods approached Baucis and Philemon's house at the beginning of "The Miraculous Pitcher"? (Response: *Zeus and Hermes.*)

2. Did Baucis and Philemon turn into trees **before** or **after** they saw a new lake? (Response: *After.*)

3. How did Baucis and Philemon treat strangers? (Idea: *Kindly.*)

4. Pretend you are reading an article about horse racing. What kinds of things would you find under the heading "Steeplechases"? (Idea: *Facts about steeplechase races.*)

5. What did the Greeks believe deities had power over? (Ideas: *The sun, the ocean, love, war, fire.*)

6. Is "Beauty and the Beast" fact or fiction? (Response: *Fiction.*)

7. How do you know "Beauty and the Beast" is fiction? (Idea: *It tells about things that never happened.*)

EXERCISE 3   Passage Reading

1. Everybody, look at the passage on page 31 of your test. You're going to read the passage aloud.

2. (Call on individual students to read several sentences each. Correct all decoding errors. When the students finish, present the following questions.)

3. At the beginning of the passage, how did Beauty and her father feel when they saw the Beast? (Idea: *Frightened.*)

4. How did Beauty act toward the Beast? (Idea: *Respectful; she tried to hide her terror.*)

5. How did her behavior affect the Beast? (Idea: *It pleased him.*)

6. With what kind of tone did the Beast speak to them? (Idea: *A tone that would have struck terror in the boldest heart.*)

7. What did the Beast say to them? (Response: *"Good evening."*)

8. What did Beauty say to the Beast? (Response: *"Good evening, Beast."*)

9. How did Beauty speak to the Beast? (Ideas: *Sweetly; bravely.*)

10. Why was the Beast pleased with Beauty? (Idea: *She seemed to have come of her own choice.*)

Retesting the Students

After you've completed the remedial exercises, retest each student individually. To administer the retest, you will need the student's original test paper, a blank copy of the test, and a red pencil. Give the student the blank copy of the test. Say, "Look at page 30. You're going to take this test again. Read each item aloud and tell me the answer."

Use the student's original test paper to grade the retest. Use the red pencil to mark each correct answer with a **C** and each incorrect answer with an **X.** Then count one point for each correct answer and write the new score at the bottom of the page. Finally, revise the Individual Skills Profile Chart by drawing an **X** over any items the student missed on the retest.

Fluency: Rate/Accuracy

Administer the fluency checkout for lesson 80. The passage begins on page 60. For further instructions, see page 52.

Tested Skills

The following list shows the test items and the skills they test.

- using vocabulary words in context (items 1–4)
- using context to predict word meaning (items 5–8)
- distinguishing settings by features (item 9)
- distinguishing characters by traits (item 10)
- sequencing narrative events (item 11)
- interpreting a character's motives (item 12)
- inferring story morals (item 13)
- making comparisons (item 14)
- identifying literal cause and effect (item 15)
- interpreting indexes and headings (item 16)
- distinguishing between fact and fiction (item 17)
- inferring the main idea (items 18 and 19)
- inferring cause and effect (item 20)
- drawing conclusions (item 21)
- relating titles to story content (item 22)
- predicting a character's actions (item 23)

LESSON 90

Administering the Test

The Lesson 90 Mastery Test should be administered after the students complete all work on lesson 90 and before they begin work on lesson 91. Each student will need a pencil and a copy of the *Curriculum-Based Assessment and Fluency Student Book.* Use the following script.

1. (Have the students clear their desks. Make sure each student has a pencil.)

2. Now you're going to take another test on what you've learned. This test will be longer than the others you've taken because it has questions about the last thirty lessons. Don't begin until I tell you.

3. Write your name on the name line.

4. Now you're ready to begin the test. Answer all the items on each page. There is no time limit. When you've finished, turn your test facedown and look up at me. Begin the test now. (If you are including the writing item as part of the testing session, tell students they can begin the writing item after they finish the mastery test.)

Grading the Test

You can grade the tests yourself, or you can have the students grade their own tests. If you want the students to grade their own tests, use the following script.

1. Now we're going to grade the test. I'll read the correct answer for each item. If the answer is correct, mark it with a **C.** If the answer is wrong, mark it with an **X.**

2. (Read the correct answers from the answer key on this page and the following.)

3. Now count the number of **correct** answers and enter the score at the end of the test.

Answer Key

Lesson 90

1. c		28. a	
2. a		29. a	
3. b		30. b	
4. c		31. c	
5. b		32. b	
6. a		33. a	
7. c		34. c	
8. a		35. b	
9. b		36. a	
10. a		37. a	
11. c		38. b	
12. a		39. b	
13. a		40. c	
14. a		41. a	
15. c		42. c	
16. b		43. b	
17. a		44. c	
18. b		45. b	
19. a		46. a	
20. b		47. c	
21. c		48. b	
22. b		49. c	
23. c		50. a	
24. c		51. b	
25. a		52. b	
26. c		53. c	
27. c			

Recording Individual Results

(Use the following script to record individual results.)

1. Look at your Individual Skills Profile Chart.

2. You're going to record your test results for lesson 90. First look at the test to find out which items you got wrong. Then circle those items on the chart.

3. Now record your results. I'll help you if you have any questions. (Circulate among the students as they record their results.)

4. (After the students finish, say:) Now count the items you did not circle and write the total in the **Total** box near the bottom of the column. The total should be the same as your test score.

5. Now you'll fill in the other boxes for lesson 90. If you scored 0 to 42 points, write an **X** in the box marked **Retest.** If you scored 43 to 53 points, write your score in the box marked **FINAL SCORE.**

Remedial Exercises

Students who scored 0 to 42 points on the test should be given remedial help. After the regular reading period is over, assemble these students and present the following exercises. The students will need their original test papers.

EXERCISE 1   Vocabulary Review

1. Let's talk about the meanings of some words.

2. The first word is **spectacular.** Something that is very impressive is **spectacular.**
   - Everybody, what's another way of saying **The very impressive mountains towered over us?** (Signal.) *The spectacular mountains towered over us.*

3. The next word is **peddler.** A **peddler** is a person who goes down the street with something to sell.
   - Everybody, what would we call a person who goes down the street selling fruit? (Signal.) *A fruit peddler.*

4. The next word is **infant. Infant** is another word for **baby.**
   - Everybody, what's another word for **baby?** (Signal.) *Infant.*

5. The next word is **supervisor.** A **supervisor** is a boss.
   - Everybody, what's another way of saying **His boss was kind?** (Signal.) *His supervisor was kind.*

6. The next word is **biography.** A **biography** is the true story of somebody's life.

   - Everybody, what's another way of saying **We read a true story of Abraham Lincoln's life?** (Signal.) *We read a biography of Abraham Lincoln.*

7. The next word is **inhabitant.** Somebody who lives in a place is an **inhabitant** of that place.
   - Everybody, what's another way of saying **José lives in a small town?** (Signal.) *José is an inhabitant of a small town.*

8. The next word is **conceal. Conceal** is another word for **hide.**
   - Everybody, what's another way of saying **My mom hid my birthday present?** (Signal.) *My mom concealed my birthday present.*

9. The next word is **portrait.** A **portrait** is a painting of a person.
   - Everybody, what's another way of saying **I have a painting of my grandmother?** (Signal.) *I have a portrait of my grandmother.*

10. The next word is **subtle.** When something is hard to see or understand, it is **subtle.**
    - Everybody, what's another way of saying **The lawyer made an argument that was hard to understand?** (Signal.) *The lawyer made a subtle argument.*

11. The next word is **agile. Agile** is another word for **nimble.**
    - Everybody, what's another way of saying **The gymnast is incredibly nimble?** (Signal.) *The gymnast is incredibly agile.*

12. The last word is **trance.** When you have a daydream or get lost in thought, you go into a **trance.**
    - Everybody, what's another way of saying **I was lost in thought in science class today?** (Signal.) *I went into a trance in science class today.*

EXERCISE 2   General Review

1. In a baseball game, what does a batter do when the ball is pitched? (Idea: *The batter tries to hit the ball to a spot where nobody on the other team can catch it*.)
2. What is it called when the batter crosses home plate? (Idea: *A run.*)
3. For what is Jackie Robinson famous? (Idea: *He was the first African American to play major-league baseball.*)

4. What did Robinson do when people called him names? (Idea: *He didn't fight back.*)

5. Which story has the lesson "Love is better than gold"? (Response: *"The Golden Touch."*)

6. What was the lesson of "The Miraculous Pitcher"? (Idea: *Be kind to strangers.*)

7. How did Beauty react to the hardships her family went through at the beginning of the story? (Idea: *She was brave and cheerful.*)

8. How did Beauty break the Beast's spell? (Idea: *She consented to marry him.*)

9. Is the poem "The Spider and the Fly" fact or fiction? (Response: *Fiction.*)

    • How do you know it's fiction? (Idea: *Spiders and flies can't talk.*)

10. In which city did Jane Addams live? (Response: *Chicago.*)

11. On what street was Hull House located? (Response: *Halsted Street.*)

12. Did Jane Addams avoid problems or try to solve them? (Idea: *She tried to solve them.*)

13. What kinds of problems did the garbage cause in Ward 19? (Ideas: *A high death rate; rats; a bad smell.*)

14. How did Jane Addams solve the garbage problem? (Idea: *She became a garbage inspector.*)

15. What country did Maria Rossi's family come from? (Response: *Italy.*)

16. What was special about Sundays in Maria's family? (Idea: *They had picnics on the beach.*)

17. What kinds of things took place at Hull House? (Idea: *Cooking and sewing classes, English classes, clubs, activities, kindergarten, art exhibits, concerts.*)

18. In the early 1930s, what was the time period called in which many people didn't have jobs? (Idea: *The Great Depression.*)

19. What big award did Jane Addams win in 1931? (Response: *The Nobel Peace Prize.*)

20. Is the biography of Jane Addams fact or fiction? (Response: *Fact.*)

EXERCISE 3   Passage Reading

Passage 1

1. Everybody, look at the passage on page 34 of your test. You're going to read the passage aloud.

2. (Call on individual students to read several sentences each. Correct all decoding errors. When the students finish, present the following questions.)

3. In what two places was Jackie Robinson supposed to be at the same time? (Ideas: *At a baseball game and a track meet.*)

4. Why did Robinson try the long jump three times? (Idea: *He wanted to see if he could do better each time.*)

5. How do you know Robinson was a fierce competitor? (Ideas: *He wanted to compete in both a track meet and a baseball game on the same day.*)

6. Why didn't Robinson stop jumping after his first or second jump? (Idea: *He thought he could do better with each jump.*)

7. Describe Robinson's performance during the baseball game. (Idea: *He got two hits and helped his team win the game.*)

8. What does the passage tell you about the kind of person Robinson was? (Ideas: *He liked challenges. He wanted to be the best at whatever he did.*)

Passage 2

1. Everybody, look at the second passage on page 35 of your test. You're going to read the passage aloud.

2. (Call on individual students to read several sentences each. Correct all decoding errors. When the students finish, present the following questions.)

3. How did Baucis feel about the meal she served the guests? (Idea: *She thought it was quite small.*)

4. Why did Quicksilver ask for more milk? (Idea: *He said he was thirsty.*)

5. Why was Baucis ashamed? (Idea: *She said there was hardly any milk left in the pitcher.*)

6. What did Quicksilver have to do with the milk? (Ideas: *He picked up the pitcher. He probably used magic to refill it.*)

7. Why is this passage not realistic? (Idea: *No one could make food multiply in real life.*)

Passage 3

1. Everybody, look at the passage on page 37 of your test. You're going to read the passage aloud.

2. (Call on individual students to read several sentences each. Correct all decoding errors. When the students finish, present the following questions.)

3. What was the day after a picnic day? (Idea: *A work day.*)

4. What is the first thing the narrator hears in the morning? (Idea: *Mama's voice.*)

5. What other noises could the narrator hear? (Ideas: *Chickens, roosters, peddlers.*)

6. How did most of the people in the neighborhood travel? (Idea: *By walking.*)

7. Why didn't many people own horses? (Idea: *They would have to keep them inside at night.*)

8. What language did the people in the neighborhood speak? (Response: *Italian.*)

9. What was the narrator's job? (Idea: *Wrapping candy.*)

10. What two colors of paper were used to wrap the candy? (Response: *Red and yellow.*)

11. What happened when the narrator wrapped the candy in the wrong color of paper? (Idea: *The foreman yelled.*)

Retesting the Students

After you've completed the remedial exercises, retest each student individually. To administer the retest, you will need the student's original test paper, a blank copy of the test, and a red pencil. Give the student the blank copy of the test. Say, "Look at page 33. You're going to take this test again. Read each item aloud and tell me the answer."

Use the student's original test paper to grade the retest. Use the red pencil to mark each correct answer with a **C** and each incorrect answer with an **X.** Then count one point for each correct answer and write the new score at the bottom of the page. Finally, revise the Individual Skills Profile Chart by drawing an **X** over any items the student missed on the retest.

Fluency: Rate/Accuracy

Administer the fluency checkout for lesson 90. The passage begins on page 61. For further instructions, see page 52.

Tested Skills

The following list shows the test items and the skills they test.

- using vocabulary words in context (items 1–6)
- using context to predict word meaning (items 7–12)
- sequencing narrative events (item 13)
- identifying literal cause and effect (items 14 and 49)
- inferring a character's point of view (items 15 and 43)
- inferring story details and events (items 16, 32, and 48)
- interpreting a character's feelings (item 34)
- distinguishing between fact and fiction (item 18)
- answering literal questions about a text (items 19 and 31)
- interpreting a character's motives (items 20 and 35)
- inferring the main idea (items 21 and 29)
- inferring details relevant to a main idea (items 22 and 30)
- relating titles to story content (items 23 and 52)
- predicting a character's actions (item 24)
- inferring story morals (item 25)
- distinguishing characters by traits (items 17, 26, and 40)
- distinguishing settings by features (items 27 and 50)
- inferring cause and effect (items 28 and 37)
- evaluating problems and solutions (items 33 and 39)
- predicting narrative outcomes (items 36 and 51)
- recalling details and events (item 38)
- drawing conclusions (items 41 and 53)
- making comparisons (item 42)
- interpreting maps (items 44 and 45)
- interpreting time lines (items 46 and 47)

LESSON 100

Administering the Test

The Lesson 100 Mastery Test should be administered after the students complete all work on lesson 100 and before they begin work on lesson 101. Each student will need a pencil and a copy of the *Curriculum-Based Assessment and Fluency Student Book.* Use the following script.

1. (Have the students clear their desks. Make sure each student has a pencil.)

2. Now you're going to take another test on what you've learned. Don't begin until I tell you.

3. Write your name on the name line.

4. Now you're ready to begin the test. Answer all the items on each page. There is no time limit. When you've finished, turn your test facedown and look up at me. Begin the test now. (If you are including the writing item as part of the testing session, tell students they can begin the writing item after they finish the mastery test.)

Grading the Test

You can grade the tests yourself, or you can have the students grade their own tests. If you want the students to grade their own tests, use the following script.

1. Now we're going to grade the test. I'll read the correct answer for each item. If the answer is correct, mark it with a **C.** If the answer is wrong, mark it with an **X.**

2. (Read the correct answers from the answer key in the next column.)

3. Now count the number of **correct** answers and enter the score at the end of the test.

Answer Key

LESSON 100

Name _____

For items 1–8, circle the letter of the answer that means the same thing as the underlined part.

1. The girl has <u>a chance</u> to win the game.
   a. the ability
   b. wisdom
   c. an opportunity *(circled)*

2. The math questions were so difficult that I felt <u>I did not understand them.</u>
   a. optimistic
   b. ignorant *(circled)*
   c. gifted

3. We saw a huge aircraft carrier at the <u>place where ships tie up.</u>
   a. harbor *(circled)*
   b. alley
   c. plumbing

4. In the park, dogs are not <u>let run free.</u>
   a. saluted
   b. unleashed *(circled)*
   c. tormented

5. The prisoner <u>was confined to</u> his cell for several years.
   a. could not leave *(circled)*
   b. disliked
   c. escaped from

6. After a good nap, my father <u>regains his senses.</u>
   a. regains the money he lost
   b. regains the respect of his friends
   c. regains the power to think clearly *(circled)*

7. There are many stories about <u>paupers</u> who work hard and become successful.
   a. people who have no money *(circled)*
   b. people born into royalty
   c. students at our school

8. The king's ball was just for <u>patricians</u> and other important people.
   a. peddlers
   b. members of the royal family *(circled)*
   c. factory owners

For items 9–23, circle the letter of the correct answer.

9. Why did many poor English farmers lose their farms in the 1500s?
   a. Rich farmers wanted more land for sheep. *(circled)*
   b. The weather was bad and crops failed.
   c. The king ordered them to stop farming.

10. Why was Queen Mary known as Bloody Mary?
    a. She always wore red.
    b. She had many people killed. *(circled)*
    c. Her favorite drink was tomato juice.

11. What was Mark Twain's first job?
    a. Newspaper reporter *(circled)*
    b. Steamboat captain
    c. Trail boss to the West

12. In *The Prince and the Pauper,* which event occured last?
    a. Tom met King Henry the Eighth. *(circled)*
    b. Tom and Edward met.
    c. Tom met Lady Jane Grey.

13. Why did the people of the palace think it was unusual for Tom to bow to them?
    a. They thought he couldn't bow while wearing heavy, jeweled clothing.
    b. They thought he had a sore leg.
    c. A prince doesn't bow to people who work for him. *(circled)*

14. Why was Tom fearful that he might be caught in the palace?
    a. Paupers were treated badly. *(circled)*
    b. He had stolen something of Edward's.
    c. He had sneaked into the palace for food.

Read the paragraph below. Then answer items 15–16.

A farmhouse in the 1500s was just a one-room wooden house with a dirt floor and a roof made out of dead branches and straw. Most had a fireplace that was used for heating and cooking. The fireplaces were often quite smoky, and the air in the farmhouse was usually pretty bad. During the winter, the family would sit around the fireplace to stay warm. They would cook soup and vegetables in pots that hung over the fire. If they were lucky, they might eat meat once a week.

15. What is the main idea of the passage?
    a. A lot of people were farmers in the 1500s.
    b. Farmers cooked in pots over a fire.
    c. Farmhouses of the 1500s were plain and simple. *(circled)*

16. What is one supporting detail for that main idea?
    a. Farmers ate a lot of vegetables.
    b. The fireplace made the house smoky.
    c. Most farmhouses had just one room. *(circled)*

17. Pretend you are reading an encyclopedia article about literature. Which heading would you look under to find information about plays?
    a. Types of literature *(circled)*
    b. Plot
    c. Oral literature

Read the passage below. Then answer items 18–23.

In London, during the year 1537, two boys were born on the same day. One boy was born to a poor family named Canty. This family did not want their boy. The other boy was born to a rich family named Tudor. This family did want their boy. In fact, everybody in England wanted him so much that they were nearly crazy with joy when he was born.

People took holidays to celebrate the birth of the Tudor boy, and they hugged people they scarcely knew. They feasted and danced and sang for days and days. And they talked and talked about the Tudor baby. For, you see, the Tudor baby was a prince—Edward Tudor, Prince of Wales, who lay wrapped in silk, with lords and ladies watching over him.

But there was no talk about the other baby, Tom Canty, who was wrapped in rags. The only people who discussed this baby were those in his family. They

weren't happy about little Tom, because they were paupers, and the presence of the baby meant more work and less food for them.

When Tom Canty grew old enough, he became a beggar. He and his family lived in a small, dilapidated house near Pudding Lane. The house was packed full of terribly poor families. Tom's family occupied a room on the third floor. His mother and father slept in a bed in a corner of the room. But Tom, his grandmother and his twin sisters, Bet and Nan, did not have beds. Instead, they slept on the floor in any place they chose. They covered themselves with the old remains of blankets or some bundles of ancient, dirty straw.

18. Why did Tom Canty become a beggar?
    a. His family had no money. *(circled)*
    b. He liked working in the street.
    c. He lost his job.

19. What kind of person was Edward Tudor's father?
    a. A pauper
    b. A knight
    c. A king *(circled)*

20. How was Tom Canty different from Edward Tudor?
    a. Tom was older.
    b. Tom was poorer. *(circled)*
    c. Tom was born in London.

21. Why was Tom's family unhappy when Tom was born?
    a. He was an ugly child.
    b. They had wanted a girl.
    c. It would cost money to feed him. *(circled)*

22. Which one of the following things might you find in Tom's house?
    a. Straw mattresses *(circled)*
    b. Marble floors
    c. Silk curtains

23. What other name did Edward Tudor have?
    a. Prince of London
    b. Prince of Wales *(circled)*
    c. Prince of Poverty

STOP—end of test—SCORE: _____

Recording Individual Results

(Use the following script to record individual results.)

1. Look at your Individual Skills Profile Chart.

2. You're going to record your test results for lesson 100. First look at the test to find out which items you got wrong. Then circle those items on the chart.

3. Now record your results. I'll help you if you have any questions. (Circulate among the students as they record their results.)

4. (After the students finish, say:) Now count the items you did not circle and write the total in the **Total** box near the bottom of the column. The total should be the same as your test score.

5. Now you'll fill in the other boxes for lesson 100. If you scored 0 to 18 points, write an **X** in the box marked **Retest.** If you scored 19 to 23 points, write your score in the box marked **FINAL SCORE.**

Remedial Exercises

Students who scored 0 to 18 points on the test should be given remedial help. After the regular reading period is over, assemble these students and present the following exercises. The students will need their original test papers.

EXERCISE 1	Vocabulary Review

1. Let's talk about the meanings of some words.

2. The first word is **hardware.** Hammers, nails, knives, and other objects made of metal are **hardware.**
- Everybody, what's another way of saying **We went to a store for metal hammers and nails?** (Signal.) *We went to a store for hardware.*

3. The next word is **opportunity.** When you have a chance to do something, you have an **opportunity** to do that thing.
- Everybody, what's another way of saying **She had a chance to go to the beach?** (Signal.) *She had an opportunity to go to the beach.*

4. The next word is **ruler.** When you are a **ruler,** you are in charge of a country.

- Everybody, what's another way of saying **The people have to obey the person in charge of their country?** (Signal.) *The people have to obey their ruler.*

5. The next word is **confined.** When you're **confined** to a place, you cannot leave that place.
- Everybody, what's another way of saying **The dog could not leave the yard?** (Signal.) *The dog was confined to the yard.*

6. The next word is **properly.** When you do things **properly,** you do them in the right way.
- Everybody, what's another way of saying **We are learning to spell words in the right way?** (Signal.) *We are learning to spell words properly.*

7. The next word is **patrician.** A **patrician** is a royal person.
- Everybody, what's another way of saying **The royal person had many servants?** (Signal.) *The patrician had many servants.*

8. The next word is **scurry. Scurry** is another word for **scamper.**
- Everybody, what's another way of saying **We saw the squirrel scamper by with nuts for the winter?** (Signal.) *We saw the squirrel scurry by with nuts for the winter.*

9. The next word is **unleash.** When you **unleash** something, you let it run free.
- Everybody, what's another way of saying **They will let the horses run free?** (Signal.) *They will unleash the horses.*

10. The next word is **identical.** When things are the same in every way, they are **identical.**
- Everybody, what's another way of saying **The birdhouses we made are the same in every way?** (Signal.) *The birdhouses we made are identical.*

11. The next word is **humorous. Humorous** is another word for **funny.**
- Everybody, what's another way of saying **The speaker told a funny story?** (Signal.) *The speaker told a humorous story.*

12. The next word is **merciful.** Someone who is not cruel is **merciful.**
- Everybody, what's another way of saying **Because it was my first ticket, the judge was not cruel?** (Signal.) *Because it was my first ticket, the judge was merciful.*

13. The last word is **foul.** When something is **foul,** it is very bad.

- Everybody, what's another way of saying **The rotting garbage smelled very bad?** (Signal.) *The rotting garbage smelled foul.*

EXERCISE 2   General Review

1. In what country does *The Prince and the Pauper* take place? (Response: *England.*)

2. When does the story take place? (Idea: *In the 1500s.*)

3. In the 1500s, what did people use fireplaces for? (Ideas: *To stay warm; to cook food.*)

4. What was Tom's job as a boy? (Idea: *He was a beggar.*)

5. At the beginning of *The Prince and the Pauper,* why was Tom a hero? (Idea: *People were astonished at his wisdom.*)

6. Everybody, look at the third paragraph of the long passage on page 41 of your test. **(Call on a student to read the paragraph.)**

- We're going to figure out the main idea of that paragraph.
- Who is the main character in the paragraph? (Idea: *Tom Canty.*)
- What was the main thing people felt about Tom Canty? (Idea: *They didn't care about him.*)
- So what is the main idea of the paragraph? (Idea: *No one cared about Tom Canty.*)

7. Name some supporting details for that main idea. (Ideas: *There was no talk about him; his family was not happy with him; his presence meant less food for his family.*)

EXERCISE 3   Passage Reading

1. Everybody, look at the long passage on page 41 of your test. You're going to read the passage aloud.

2. (Call on individual students to read several sentences each. Correct all decoding errors. When the students finish, present the following questions.)

3. How much money did Tom's family have? (Idea: *None.*)

4. So what did Tom have to do to help his family? (Idea: *He had to beg.*)

5. What kind of royal person was Edward Tudor? (Idea: *A prince.*)

6. So what kind of royal person was Edward's mother? (Idea: *A queen.*)

7. Which boy—Tom or Edward—was richer? (Response: *Edward.*)

8. Which boy—Tom or Edward—was hungrier? (Response: *Tom.*)

9. Why were people happy when Edward was born? (Ideas: *He was a prince; he would be king someday.*)

10. Name some things you would find in Tom's house. (Ideas: *Poor people; old blankets; dirty straw.*)

11. What was Edward's last name? (Response: *Tudor.*)

12. What was Tom's last name? (Response: *Canty.*)

Retesting the Students

After you've completed the remedial exercises, retest each student individually. To administer the retest, you will need the student's original test paper, a blank copy of the test, and a red pencil. Give the student the blank copy of the test. Say, "Look at page 40. You're going to take this test again. Read each item aloud and tell me the answer."

Use the student's original test paper to grade the retest. Use the red pencil to mark each correct answer with a **C** and each incorrect answer with an **X.** Then count one point for each correct answer and write the new score at the bottom of the page. Finally, revise the Individual Skills Profile Chart by drawing an **X** over any items the student missed on the retest.

Fluency: Rate/Accuracy

Administer the fluency checkout for lesson 100. The passage begins on page 62. For further instructions, see page 52.

Tested Skills

The following list shows the test items and the skills they test.

- using vocabulary words in context (items 1–4)
- using context to predict word meaning (items 5–8)
- identifying literal cause and effect (item 9)
- distinguishing characters by traits (item 10)
- recalling details and events (item 11)
- sequencing narrative events (item 12)
- inferring story details and events (item 13)
- interpreting a character's feelings (item 14)
- inferring the main idea (item 15)
- inferring details relevant to a main idea (item 16)
- interpreting indexes and headings (item 17)
- inferring cause and effect (item 18)
- drawing conclusions (item 19)
- making comparisons (item 20)
- inferring a character's point of view (item 21)
- distinguishing settings by features (item 22)
- answering literal questions about a text (item 23)

LESSON 110

Administering the Test

The Lesson 110 Mastery Test should be administered after the students complete all work on lesson 110 and before they begin work on lesson 111. Each student will need a pencil and a copy of the *Curriculum-Based Assessment and Fluency Student Book.* Use the following script.

1. (Have the students clear their desks. Make sure each student has a pencil.)

2. Now you're going to take another test on what you've learned. Don't begin until I tell you.

3. Write your name on the name line.

4. Now you're ready to begin the test. Answer all the items on each page. There is no time limit. When you've finished, turn your test facedown and look up at me. Begin the test now. (If you are including the writing item as part of the testing session, tell students they can begin the writing item after they finish the mastery test.)

Grading the Test

You can grade the tests yourself, or you can have the students grade their own tests. If you want the students to grade their own tests, use the following script.

1. Now we're going to grade the test. I'll read the correct answer for each item. If the answer is correct, mark it with a **C**. If the answer is wrong, mark it with an **X**.

2. (Read the correct answers from the answer key in the next column.)

3. Now count the number of **correct** answers and enter the score at the end of the test.

Answer Key

LESSON 110

Name _____

For items 1–8, circle the letter of the answer that means the same thing as the underlined part.

1. The stout and strong cowboy held on to the bull.
   - (a.) burly
   - b. drowsy
   - c. motley

2. In the far north, winter is a difficult experience.
   - a. vast
   - b. charred
   - (c.) an ordeal

3. The ball went through the window and broke it into hundreds of pieces.
   - a. misplaced
   - (b.) shattered
   - c. shuddered

4. The queen liked her bed sprinkled with a perfume made of water and roses.
   - (a.) rose water
   - b. a seal
   - c. a clothesline

5. When the teacher assisted me, I was able to solve the problem.
   - (a.) helped
   - b. scolded
   - c. ignored

6. No one likes a person who is always irritable.
   - (a.) grouchy
   - b. friendly
   - c. quiet

7. Liz put her broken arm into a sling.
   - a. plaster cast
   - b. bandage
   - (c.) loop of cloth

8. Don't sleep late and run the risk of being late for school.
   - (a.) take the chance
   - b. make fun
   - c. look into the camera

For items 9–23, circle the letter of the correct answer.

9. What would a king probably not know how to do?
   - a. Order servants to bring him dinner
   - (b.) Cook breakfast for himself
   - c. Make someone into a knight

10. Where did the gang of thieves hide out?
    - a. John Canty's house
    - b. The palace
    - (c.) A barn

11. Why did the gang of robbers make fun of Edward?
    - a. He was such a small boy.
    - b. His clothes were torn.
    - (c.) He said he was the king.

12. Which event occurred last?
    - a. King Henry died.
    - (b.) Tom became King.
    - c. Tom and Edward changed places.

13. What was Humphry Marlow's job?
    - a. He served Edward breakfast.
    - b. He cleaned Edward's socks.
    - (c.) He was Edward's whipping boy.

14. What might have happened if Edward hadn't escaped the troop of ruffians?
    - a. He might have turned them in to the king.
    - (b.) He might have been caught and whipped.
    - c. He might have convinced them to change their ways.

Read the passage below. Then answer items 15–17.

As the rain continued, the gang started to make merry. They shouted and cackled and sang loud songs. One of the blind men got up and took off the patches that covered his excellent eyes. He tossed aside the sign that told how he had lost his eyesight. Another member of the gang removed a wooden leg. Underneath was a perfectly healthy limb. The blind man and the man with the wooden leg joined the others in roaring out the words of a song.

15. What is the main idea of the passage?
    - a. The gang sings when it rains.
    - (b.) Some of the gang were pretending to be disabled.
    - c. In the 1500s, people made artificial legs from wood.

16. What is one supporting detail for that main idea?
    - a. The gang sang loudly.
    - b. A wooden leg was removable.
    - (c.) Two men removed their disguises.

17. What is the most likely reason the men pretended to be disabled?
    - (a.) Disguises are helpful for thieves.
    - b. They were going to a costume party.
    - c. They wanted to protect their eyes and legs.

Read the passage below. Then answer items 18–23.

A man stood up and stripped away some of his rags. He showed his back, which was crisscrossed with thick old scars left by a whip. There was also a large V that had been branded on his shoulder.

The man said, "I am Yokel. Once I was a farmer who prospered. I had a loving wife and children. You can see that I'm different now. My wife and children are gone. They're lucky because they don't have to live in England any more. My mother tried to earn a little bread by nursing the sick. One of the people she nursed died, and the doctors did not know why. So they put her in prison."

Yokel shook his head and yelled loudly, "English law! Let's cheer for that fine English law!" His voice was bitter as he continued. "After I could not farm, I started to beg. But you know it's against English law to beg. My wife and I went from house to house with our hungry children until they caught us. They lashed us through three towns. Another cheer for English law!"

Yokel continued. "My wife died after the last lashing, and my children starved. Those children never harmed any creature, but now they are gone. Then I begged again, just for a crust of bread. When they caught me, I was sold for a slave. A slave! Do you understand that word? I am an English slave, and when I'm found, I shall hang. Another cheer for English law!"

18. How did Yokel's mother earn money?
    - a. Farming
    - b. Begging
    - (c.) Nursing the sick

19. What does the brand V probably mean?
    - a. Violin player
    - b. Violent
    - (c.) Vagrant

20. How did Yokel feel about English Law?
    - (a.) He thought it was horrible.
    - b. He thought it was fair.
    - c. He thought it was too complicated.

21. What will Yokel probably do next?
    - a. Become a lawyer
    - (b.) Go to another town and beg
    - c. Try to become a farmer again

22. Why did Yokel cheer for the English law?
    - a. He thought England should make more people into slaves.
    - b. He agreed that begging should be against the law.
    - (c.) He was being sarcastic.

23. If somebody died for an unknown reason, how did English law try to solve the problem?
    - (a.) Put the person's nurse in prison
    - b. Give doctors more training
    - c. Give people free medicine

STOP—end of test—SCORE: _____

Recording Individual Results

(Use the following script to record individual results.)

1. Look at your Individual Skills Profile Chart.

2. You're going to record your test results for lesson 110. First look at the test to find out which items you got wrong. Then circle those items on the chart.

3. Now record your results. I'll help you if you have any questions. (Circulate among the students as they record their results.)

4. (After the students finish, say:) Now count the items you did not circle and write the total in the **Total** box near the bottom of the column. The total should be the same as your test score.

5. Now you'll fill in the other boxes for lesson 110. If you scored 0 to 18 points, write an **X** in the box marked **Retest.** If you scored 19 to 23 points, write your score in the box marked **FINAL SCORE.**

Remedial Exercises

Students who scored 0 to 18 points on the test should be given remedial help. After the regular reading period is over, assemble these students and present the following exercises. The students will need their original test papers.

EXERCISE 1   Vocabulary Review

1. Let's talk about the meanings of some words.

2. The first word is **burly. Burly** means "stout and strong."
- Everybody, what's another way of saying **The stout and strong police officer helped lift the car?** (Signal.) *The burly police officer helped lift the car.*

3. The next word is **drowsy. Drowsy** is another word for **sleepy.**
- Everybody, what's another way of saying **The woman felt sleepy after the big meal?** (Signal.) *The woman felt drowsy after the big meal.*

4. The next word is **shudder. Shudder** is another word for shiver.
- Everybody, what's another way of saying **The**

children shivered in the cold? (Signal.) *The children shuddered in the cold.*

5. The next word is **ordeal.** An **ordeal** is a difficult experience.
- Everybody, what's another way of saying **The trip was a difficult experience?** (Signal.) *The trip was an ordeal.*

6. The next word is **assist.** When you **assist** somebody, you help that person.
- Everybody, what's another way of saying **The conductor helped people onto the train?** (Signal.) *The conductor assisted people onto the train.*

7. The next word is **irritable.** When you are **irritable,** you are grouchy.
- Everybody, what's another way of saying **The grouchy boy had few friends?** (Signal.) *The irritable boy had few friends.*

8. The next word is **butler.** A **butler** is a male servant who is in charge of other servants.
- Everybody, what's another way of saying **The male servant opened the door for the king?** (Signal.) *The butler opened the door for the king.*

9. The next word is **stout.** When something is thick and sturdy, it is **stout.**
- Everybody, what's another way of saying **We made thick, sturdy legs for the table?** (Signal.) *We made stout legs for the table.*

10. The next word is **withdraw.** When you take something back, you **withdraw** that thing.
- Everybody, what's another way of saying **May I take back my offer to help today?** (Signal.) *May I withdraw my offer to help today?*

11. The next word is **vagrant.** A **vagrant** is a person who doesn't have a place to live and has no job.
- Everybody, what's another way of saying **Anyone who doesn't have a job or a place to live can get a meal here?** (Signal.) *A vagrant can get a meal here.*

12. The next word is **retreat.** When you **retreat,** you move back.
- Everybody, what's another way of saying **The troops moved back to the forest?** (Signal.) *The troops retreated to the forest.*

13. The last word is **regret.** When you **regret,** you are sorry about something that happened.

- Everybody, what's another way of saying **I am sorry I broke the dish?** (Signal.) *I regret I broke the dish.*

EXERCISE 2 — General Review

1. Who made Miles Hendon a knight? (Response: *Edward.*)

2. What special request did Miles make when Edward knighted him? (Idea: *He wanted to sit in the king's presence.*)

3. What was the name of Miles's brother? (Response: *Hugh Hendon.*)

4. Would a king be likely to mop his own floors? (Response: *No.*)

- Why not? (Idea: *His servants would mop the floors.*)

5. Who was King Foo-Foo the First? (Response: *Edward.*)

6. Why did John Canty think Edward was crazy? (Idea: *Edward claimed himself to be the king.*)

7. When Edward was growing up, who was punished when Edward made mistakes? (Ideas: *Humphry Marlow; his whipping boy.*)

EXERCISE 3 — Passage Reading

1. Everybody, look at the long passage on page 44 of your test. You're going to read the passage aloud.

2. (Call on individual students to read several sentences each. Correct all decoding errors. When the students finish, present the following questions.)

3. What caused the scars on Yokel's back? (Idea: *A whip.*)

4. What was the mark on his shoulder? (Idea: *A large V.*)

5. What had been his occupation? (Idea: *A farmer.*)

6. Why did Yokel say his wife and children were lucky? (Idea: *They were gone and didn't have to live in England anymore.*)

7. Why was Yokel's mother put in prison? (Idea: *One of the people she nursed died, and the doctors did not know why.*)

8. What happened when Yokel and his family were caught begging? (Idea: *They were lashed.*)

9. What happened to Yokel's wife after the last lashing? (Idea: *She died.*)

10. What happened to Yokel's children? (Idea: *They starved.*)

11. Why was Yokel sold for a slave? (Idea: *He was caught begging for a crust of bread.*)

Retesting the Students

After you've completed the remedial exercises, retest each student individually. To administer the retest, you will need the student's original test paper, a blank copy of the test, and a red pencil. Give the student the blank copy of the test. Say, "Look at page 43. You're going to take this test again. Read each item aloud and tell me the answer."

Use the student's original test paper to grade the retest. Use the red pencil to mark each correct answer with a **C** and each incorrect answer with an **X.** Then count one point for each correct answer and write the new score at the bottom of the page. Finally, revise the Individual Skills Profile Chart by drawing an **X** over any items the student missed on the retest.

Fluency: Rate/Accuracy

Administer the fluency checkout for lesson 110. The passage begins on page 63. For further instructions, see page 52.

Tested Skills

The following list shows the test items and the skills they test.
- using vocabulary words in context (items 1–4)
- using context to predict word meaning (items 5–8)
- drawing conclusions (item 9)
- distinguishing settings by features (item 10)
- identifying literal cause and effect (item 11)
- sequencing narrative events (item 12)
- recalling details and events (item 13)
- predicting narrative outcomes (item 14)
- inferring the main idea (item 15)
- inferring details relevant to a main idea (item 16)
- inferring cause and effect (item 17)
- answering literal questions about a text (item 18)
- inferring story details and events (item 19)
- interpreting a character's feelings (item 20)
- predicting a character's actions (item 21)
- interpreting a character's motives (item 22)
- evaluating problems and solutions (item 23)

LESSON 120

Administering the Test

The Lesson 120 Mastery Test should be administered after the students complete all work on lesson 120. Each student will need a pencil and a copy of the *Curriculum-Based Assessment and Fluency Student Book.* Use the following script.

1. (Have the students clear their desks. Make sure each student has a pencil.)

2. Now you're going to take another test on what you've learned. This test will be longer than the others you've taken because it has questions about the last thirty lessons. Don't begin until I tell you.

3. Write your name on the name line.

4. Now you're ready to begin the test. Answer all the items on each page. There is no time limit. When you've finished, turn your test facedown and look up at me. Begin the test now. (If you are including the writing item as part of the testing session, tell students they can begin the writing item after they finish the mastery test.)

Grading the Test

You can grade the test yourself, or you can have the students grade their own tests. If you want the students to grade their own tests, use the following script.

1. Now we're going to grade the test. I'll read the correct answer for each item. If the answer is correct, mark it with a **C.** If the answer is wrong, mark it with an **X.**

2. (Read the correct answers from the answer key on this page and the following.)

3. Now count the number of **correct** answers and enter the score at the end of the test.

Answer Key

Lesson 120

1. b		25. a	
2. a		26. c	
3. b		27. c	
4. c		28. b	
5. c		29. a	
6. a		30. b	
7. a		31. b	
8. a		32. b	
9. b		33. a	
10. a		34. c	
11. b		35. c	
12. a		36. a	
13. c		37. b	
14. a		38. c	
15. c		39. a	
16. a		40. a	
17. b		41. a	
18. c		42. c	
19. a		43. a	
20. c		44. a	
21. c		45. b	
22. b		46. c	
23. a		47. a	
24. c		48. b	

Recording Individual Results

(Use the following script to record individual results.)

1. Look at your Individual Skills Profile Chart.

2. You're going to record your test results for lesson 120. First look at the test to find out which items you got wrong. Then circle those items on the chart.

3. Now record your results. I'll help you if you have any questions. (Circulate among the students as they record their results.)

4. (After the students finish, say:) Now count the items you did not circle and write the total in the **Total** box near the bottom of the column. The total should be the same as your test score.

5. Now you'll fill in the other boxes for lesson 120. If you scored 0 to 38 points, write an **X** in the box marked **Retest.** If you scored 39 to 48 points, write your score in the box marked **FINAL SCORE.**

Remedial Exercises

Students who scored 0 to 38 points on the test should be given remedial help. After the regular reading period is over, assemble these students and present the following exercises. The students will need their original test papers.

EXERCISE 1   Vocabulary Review
---

1. Let's talk about the meanings of some words.

2. The first word is **hustle.** When you **hustle,** you move fast.
 • Everybody, what's another way of saying **When the bell rang, we moved fast to class?** (Signal.) *When the bell rang, we hustled to class.*

3. The next word is **craft. Craft** is another word for **boat.**
 • Everybody, what's another way of saying **We sailed the boat toward the dock.** (Signal.) *We sailed the craft toward the dock.*

4. The next word is **grave.** One meaning of **grave** is **serious.**
 • Everybody, what's another way of saying **She made a serious mistake on the test?** (Signal.) *She made a grave mistake on the test.*

5. The next word is **inspect.** When you **inspect** something, you look at it closely.
 • Everybody, what's another way of saying **The doctor looked at my eye closely?** (Signal.) *The doctor inspected my eye.*

6. The next word is **pester.** Another word for **pester** is **annoy.**
 • Everybody, what's another way of saying **Your tapping is annoying me?** (Signal.) *Your tapping is pestering me.*

7. The next word is **hospitable.** When you treat guests kindly, you are **hospitable** to them.
 • Everybody, what's another way of saying **My uncle treats guests kindly?** (Signal.) *My uncle is hospitable.*

8. The next word is **slumber. Slumber** is another word for **sleep.**
 • Everybody, what's another way of saying **Students never sleep in school?** (Signal.) *Students never slumber in school.*

9. The next word is **imposter.** Someone who pretends to be somebody else is an imposter.
 • Everybody, what's an imposter? (Signal.) *Someone who pretends to be somebody else.*

10. The next word is **motley.** When something is **motley,** it is made up of many different types of things.
 • Everybody, what's another way of saying **Suzy had a motley collection of insects?** (Signal.) *Suzy had a collection of many different types of insects.*

11. The next word is **prosper.** When you **prosper,** you earn money and do well.
 • Everybody, what's another way of saying **The man earned money and did well?** (Signal.) *The man prospered.*

12. The next word is **tragic.** Something that is **tragic** is very sad.
 • Everybody, what's another way of saying **The play had a very sad ending?** (Signal.) *The play had a tragic ending.*

13. The next word is **intend. Intend** is another word for **plan.**
 • Everybody, what's another way of saying **I plan to get a good grade?** (Signal.) *I intend to get a good grade.*

14. The last word is **overcast.** When the sky is gray and cloudy, it is **overcast.**
 • Everybody, what's another way of saying **We hope the gray and cloudy sky doesn't mean rain?** (Signal.) *We hope the overcast sky doesn't mean rain.*

1. If the people in the 1500s had no plumbing, no gas, and no electricity, how did they cook and keep warm? (Idea: *They used fireplaces.*)

2. London had a busy harbor. What comes in to a harbor? (Idea: *Ships.*)

3. What did a king wear on his head to show that he was the ruler of England? (Idea: *A crown.*)

4. Why did so many poor farmers lose their land to rich farmers? (Idea: *The rich farmers took the land for their sheep.*)

5. In the first chapter of The Prince and the Pauper; what were the people celebrating? (Idea: *The birth of Edward Tudor.*)

6. What is rose water? (Idea: *Perfume made of water and roses.*)

7. At the Mayor's banquet, what did it mean when the prince drank from the golden cup? (Idea: *The banquet had begun.*)

8. When did the whipping boy get whipped? (Idea: *When the prince did poorly in his studies.*)

9. What had King Henry misplaced before he died? (Idea: *The royal seal.*)

10. What did the gang of vagrants call Edward? (Idea: *Foo-Foo the First.*)

11. How did the widow test Edward? (Ideas: *She asked him questions about different subjects; she left hotcakes on the stove.*)

12. What did the woman have in the basket that Hugo tried to steal? (Idea: *Ham.*)

13. How did Miles convince the officer to let him and Edward escape? (Idea: *Miles threatened to tell the judge how the officer cheated the woman.*)

14. Who was living in Hendon Hall when Miles and Edward arrived there? (Idea: *Hugh and Edith.*)

Passage 1

1. Everybody, look at the passage on page 47 of your test. You're going to read the passage aloud.

2. (Call on individual students to read several sentences each. Correct all decoding errors. When the students finish, present the following questions.)

3. What time of day was it when Edward was wandering? (Idea: *Night.*)

4. Why could Edward hardly walk? (Idea: *His feet were sore.*)

5. What was Edward's plan for getting back to the palace? (Idea: *He would explain his situation to Tom's parents, and they would take him back to the palace.*)

6. Why did the lights in the houses begin to twinkle? (Idea: *The people were lighting their lamps.*)

7. Why was John Canty angry at Edward? (Idea: *Edward hadn't brought the family anything.*)

8. What did Edward ask John Canty to do? (Idea: *Take him to the palace.*)

9. What did John Canty think Edward was doing? (Idea: *Playing games with him.*)

Passage 2

1. Everybody, look at the passage on page 48 of your test. You're going to read the passage aloud.

2. (Call on individual students to read several sentences each. Correct all decoding errors. When the students finish, present the following questions.)

3. When did Tom eat dinner? (Idea: *After one in the afternoon.*)

4. Where did Tom eat dinner? (Idea: *A fancy dining room.*)

5. Who besides Tom was in the room? (Idea: *Servants.*)

6. What does the Lord Chief Diaperer help Tom with? (Idea: *He puts a napkin around Tom's neck.*)

7. What was the Taster prepared to do? (Idea: *Taste any dish.*)

8. How did the servants react to Tom's odd behavior? (Idea: *With no surprise.*)

Passage 3

1. Everybody, look at the long passage on pages 49 and 50 of your test. You're going to read the passage aloud.

2. (Call on individual students to read several sentences each. Correct all decoding errors. When the students finish, present the following questions.)

3. Everybody, look again at the first two paragraphs of the passage. (Call on a student to reread the first two paragraphs.)
- Who are the main characters in those paragraphs? (Idea: *Tom and his mother.*)
- What is the main thing they do? (Idea: *Find each other.*)
- So what's the main idea? (Idea: *Tom and his mother found each other.*)

4. Name some supporting details for that main idea. (Ideas: *Tom recognized his mother; Tom waved to his mother; Tom's mother embraced him.*)

5. Why was the woman happy when she saw Tom? (Idea: *He was her son.*)

6. So what did she do? (Idea: *Ran toward him.*)

7. What did Tom say to her? (Idea: *I do not know you.*)

8. How did Tom feel about what he said? (Idea: *Ashamed.*)

9. What would probably happen if Tom let his mother ride next to him? (Ideas: *The procession would stop; everyone would be confused.*)

10. Why did Hertford want Tom to keep smiling? (Idea: *He wanted to keep things running smoothly.*)

11. What was the first feeling that Tom had? (Idea: *Enjoyment.*)

Retesting the Students

After you've completed the remedial exercises, retest each student individually.

Fluency: Rate/Accuracy

Administer the fluency checkout for lesson 120. The passage begins on page 64. For further instructions, see page 52.

Tested Skills

The following list shows the test items and the skills they test.
- using vocabulary words in context (items 1–6)
- using context to predict word meaning (items 7–12)
- sequencing narrative events (items 13, 30, and 47)
- identifying literal cause and effect (item 14)
- inferring a character's point of view (items 24 and 28)
- inferring story details and events (item 46)
- interpreting a character's feelings (items 16, 33, and 44)
- using an index (item 18)
- answering literal questions about a text (items 21, 31, and 32)
- interpreting a character's motives (items 27 and 43)
- inferring the main idea (items 19 and 40)
- inferring details relevant to a main idea (items 20 and 41)
- relating titles to story content (item 36)
- predicting a character's actions (items 23 and 45)
- distinguishing characters by traits (items 15 and 25)
- distinguishing settings by features (items 26 and 35)
- inferring cause and effect (items 22, 34, and 42)
- predicting narrative outcomes (item 48)
- recalling details and events (items 17 and 39)
- drawing conclusions (item 37)
- making comparisons (items 29 and 38)

Guidelines for Evaluating Writing Items

General Guidelines

Did the student
- indent the paragraph?
- write in complete sentences?
- begin each sentence with a capital letter and end it with appropriate punctuation?
- spell most words correctly?
- stick to the subject?
- answer the questions or follow the directions in the prompt?

Scoring

If you wish to score the writing items, use the general guidelines listed above along with the following scoring guide:

0 The student wrote nothing.

1 The student wrote something but did not answer any of the questions or respond to any of the issues raised in the prompt.

2 The student answered some of the questions and responded to some of the issues raised in the prompt.

3 The student answered all the questions and responded to all the issues raised in the prompt.

Specific Guidelines

Lesson 10, Item 19
Did the student answer the following questions in the prompt?
- How did Ron learn to paddle a kayak?
- What did Ron do when he saw the rapids?
- How did Ron paddle through the rapids?

Did the student write at least four sentences?

Lesson 20, Item 19
Did the student answer the following questions in the prompt?
- What does the character look like?
- How does the character behave?
- What does the character want?
- How does the character treat other characters?

Lesson 30, Item 49
Did the student answer the following questions in the prompt?
- How were Ron's and Dorothy's journeys alike?
- How were their journeys different?
- How were the endings of the two stories alike?

Lesson 40, Item 19
Did the student follow the directions in the prompt? Did the student include likely things a mother would say to a child who had been picked on?

Lesson 50, Item 19
Did the student follow the directions in the prompt? Did the student describe (rather than just name) three geographical features in the area?

Lesson 60, Item 54
Did the student follow the directions in the prompt? Did the student tell where wild animals sleep and where pets sleep? Did the student tell what wild animals eat and what pets eat? Did the student tell how wild animals protect themselves and how pets protect themselves? Did the student tell how wild animals behave toward people and how pets behave toward people?

Lesson 70, Item 23
Did the student follow the directions in the prompt?
- Tell the rules of a sport or game.
- Give reasons for the rules and tell what would happen if the rules didn't exist.

Lesson 80, Item 24
Did the student follow the directions in the prompt?
- Why should people be kind to others?
- What kinds of things can we do to help others?
- Does kindness benefit the giver or the receiver more?

Lesson 90, Item 54
Did the student follow the directions in the prompt?
- Tell what activities and services his or her neighborhood needs.

Lesson 100, Item 24
Did the student follow the directions in the prompt?
- Tell how cooking is done in the present time.
- Tell how cooking and foods in your own time are different from cooking and foods in the 1500s?

Lesson 110, Item 24
Did the student follow the directions in the prompt?
- What rules would there be for behavior? For dress?
- What are the rules for the family? For guests?

Lesson 120, Item 49
Did the student follow the directions in the prompt?
- Did the student write questions to ask about being an astronaut?

Fluency: Rate/Accuracy

The assessments measure comprehension, literary appreciation, and study skills. Decoding skills are measured by the individual fluency checkouts. For an individual fluency checkout, a student reads a passage aloud as you count decoding errors. Students earn points for reading the passage accurately. A fluency checkout takes about a minute and a half per student. Checkouts should be administered in a corner of the classroom so that the other students won't overhear.

Procedure

The student will read the passage for that lesson. The shaded portion in your answer key shows the amount of words the student must read. The student may read further if able to. Use the following procedure.

1. Tell the student to look at the passage lesson being assessed.

2. Note the time and tell the student to begin reading the passage.

3. As the student reads, make a tally mark on a sheet of paper for each decoding error the student makes. (See below for a complete description of decoding errors.)

4. At the end of one minute, tell the student to stop reading.

5. Record student performance as total time over number of errors in the appropriate box on the Individual Fluency: Rate/Accuracy Chart.

Decoding Error Guidelines

- If the student misreads a word, count one error.

- If the student omits a word ending, such as s or ed, count one error.

- If the student reads a word incorrectly and then correctly, count one error.

- If the student sounds out a word instead of reading it normally, count one error.

- If the student does not identify a word within three seconds, tell the student the word and count one error.

- If the student skips a word, count one error.

- If the student skips a line, point to the line and count one error.

- If the student does not finish the passage within the given time limit, count every word not read as an error. For example, if the student is eight words from the end of the passage at the end of the time limit, count eight errors.

The first few feet of the rapids weren't that bad. Ron's kayak   **12**
stayed in the middle, far from the rocks along the edge. But then   **25**
the rapids narrowed and the water moved even faster. Ron looked   **36**
ahead and saw a huge boulder sticking out of the middle of the   **49**
river. Half the river flowed around the right side of the boulder, and   **62**
the other half flowed around the left.   **69**

      Both sides looked dangerous, with the water spraying high   **78**
into the air and roaring loudly. Ron decided to try for the right side   **92**
of the boulder. Using all his strength, he made several quick   **103**
strokes on the left side of the kayak. Nothing happened. He was   **115**
still going in a straight line, and he was headed directly toward the   **128**
boulder!   **129**

      Ron quickly moved his paddle over to the right. He was only   **141**
a few feet from the boulder, and he had to turn fast. He grabbed   **155**
the handle as hard as he could, and he paddled furiously. At the   **168**
last second, the kayak turned left and swept around the left side   **180**
of the boulder, with only inches to spare.   **188**

      Now Ron was really frightened. He was going many times   **198**
faster than when he had started, back in the calm part of the river.   **212**
His kayak was filling with cold water, and he was soaking wet from   **225**
all the spray. He could just barely see the boulder as he swept   **238**
around it, carried along by the current.   **245**

      Ron felt as if he were zooming down a huge, curving   **256**
playground slide. But the slide didn't seem to have any end, and   **268**
Ron had no idea where he was headed.   **276**

The travelers walked along listening to the singing of the   **10**
bright-colored birds and looking at the lovely flowers, which now   **20**
became so thick that the ground was covered with them.   **30**

"Aren't they beautiful?" Dorothy asked as she breathed in   **39**
the spicy scent of the flowers.   **45**

"I always did like flowers," said the Lion. "They seem so   **56**
helpless. But there are none in the forest as bright as these."   **68**

Now, when there are many of these scarlet flowers together,   **78**
their odor is so powerful that anyone who breathes them falls   **89**
asleep; and if the sleeper is not carried away from the flowers, he   **102**
sleeps on forever. But Dorothy did not know this, nor could she   **114**
get away from the flowers.   **119**

Her eyes soon grew heavy, and she felt she must sit down to   **132**
rest and sleep.   **135**

But the Tin Woodman would not let her do this.   **145**

"We must hurry and get back to the yellow brick road before   **157**
dark," he said. So they kept walking until Dorothy could stand no   **169**
longer. Her eyes closed, and she forgot where she was, and she   **181**
fell among the flowers, fast asleep.   **187**

"What shall we do?" asked the Tin Woodman.   **195**

"If we leave her here, she will die," said the Lion. "The smell   **208**
of the flowers is killing us all. I can scarcely keep my eyes open,   **222**
and the dog is asleep already."   **228**

It was true—Toto had fallen down beside his mistress. But   **239**
the Scarecrow and the Tin Woodman, since they weren't made of   **250**
flesh, were not troubled by the odor of the flowers.   **260**

Ron looked down the river to see where he was headed. He   **12**
couldn't see very far ahead, because a bend in the river blocked   **24**
his view. But Ron could hear the sound of roaring rapids. He   **36**
guessed that the rapids started soon after the bend in the river.   **48**

    The sound of the rapids made Ron's heart beat faster, and it   **60**
also made him a little afraid. He wondered how well he could   **72**
paddle through the rapids, so he examined his kayak closely. It   **83**
was a small plastic kayak, with just one seat in the middle, where   **96**
Ron was sitting.   **99**

The inside of the kayak was completely empty: no food, no   **110**
maps, no supplies of any kind. For a moment, the lack of supplies   **123**
made Ron glad because nothing would get wet or lost if the kayak   **136**
tipped over.   **138**

    The next moment, however, Ron started to worry about his   **148**
lack of supplies. What if he got hungry? What if he got lost? What   **162**
if night fell and he didn't have any light or anywhere to sleep?   **175**
What if there were bears?   **180**

LESSON 40

Later that day, the mother and her ducklings went down to a | **12**
clearing by the river. Some full-grown ducks were swimming in the | **23**
river, and others were waddling around and quacking in chorus. | **33**

One large duck quacked much louder than the rest, and | **43**
when he saw the ugly duckling, he said, in a voice that seemed to | **57**
echo, "I have never seen anything as ugly as that great tall | **69**
duckling. He is a disgrace. I shall go and chase him away." And he | **83**
ran up to the brown duckling and bit his neck, making a small | **96**
bruise. | **97**

The ugly duckling gave out a loud quack because this was | **108**
the first time he had felt any pain. His mother turned around | **120**
quickly. | **121**

"Leave him alone," she said fiercely to the loud duck. "What | **132**
has he done to you?" | **137**

"Nothing," answered the duck. "He is just so disgusting that | **147**
I can't stand him!" | **151**

Although the ugly duckling did not understand the meaning | **160**
of the loud duck's words, he felt he was being blamed for | **172**
something. He became even more uncomfortable when the loud | **181**
duck said, "It certainly is a great shame that he is so different from | **195**
the rest of us. Too bad he can't be hatched again." | **206**

The poor little fellow dropped his head and did not know | **217**
what to do, but he was comforted when his mother answered, "He | **229**
may not be quite as handsome as the others, but he swims with | **242**
ease, and he is very strong. I am sure he will make his way in the | **258**
world as well as anybody." | **263**

"I doubt it," said the loud duck as he waddled off. | **274**

LESSON 50

The crowd fell silent. Everybody knew that Buck was a 10
magnificent animal; but the thousand pounds of flour was more 20
than any dog could pull. 25

Thornton knelt by Buck's side. He took the dog's head in his 37
two hands and rested his cheek on Buck's cheek. He did not 49
playfully shake him or murmur softly. But he whispered something 59
in the dog's ear. Buck whined eagerly. 66

The crowd was watching curiously. The affair was growing 75
mysterious. It seemed like a magic trick. As Thornton got to his 87
feet, Buck seized Thornton's hand between his jaws, pressing in 97
with his teeth and releasing slowly. It was Buck's answer. 107

Thornton stepped back. "Now, Buck," he said. 114

Buck pulled his harness tight, then let it slacken a bit. 125

"Gee!" Thornton's voice rang out, sharp in the tense silence. 135

Buck followed the command. He swung to the right, ending 145
the movement in a lunge that jerked the harness and stopped his 157
one hundred and fifty pounds. The load quivered, and a crisp 168
crackling rose from under the runners. 174

"Haw!" Thornton commanded. 177

Buck made the same move, this time to the left. The 188
crackling turned into a snapping. The sled turned slightly, and the 199
runners slipped and grated several inches to the side. The sled 210
was broken out. Men were holding their breath. 218

"Now, MUSH ON!" 221

Tara's father had told her that the Briggs family might have to | **12**
get rid of Nellie. As Tara prepared for bed that night, she felt | **25**
discouraged. She kept thinking about possible ideas for keeping | **34**
Nellie inside the pasture, but all the ideas cost money. Nellie | **45**
couldn't stay tied up in her stall all day, but if Nellie was left alone | **60**
in the pasture . . . | **66**

Tara got into bed and tried to sleep, but Nellie kept popping | **78**
into her mind. And every time she thought about Nellie, Tara | **89**
remembered the instant she first saw her leaping the fence. | **99**

Tara punched her pillow, rolled over angrily, and told herself | **109**
that she had to come up with a solution to the problem. Suddenly, | **122**
she sat upright in bed with a smile. An idea came to her with such | **137**
force that she wondered why she hadn't thought of it before. "No | **149**
horse can jump like that," she said aloud. "She's probably the | **160**
greatest jumping horse in the world." | **166**

Tara had to resist the impulse to jump out of bed and tell her | **180**
parents of the plan that was forming in her mind. But she | **192**
controlled herself, thinking, "I'll get all the facts first, and then I'll | **204**
tell them about it." | **208**

The morning after Tara got her marvelous idea, she woke up | **219**
very early, when the sky was still dark, with just a hint of light | **233**
along the horizon to the east. Tara was up early because she | **245**
wanted to find out about jumping horses. | **252**

LESSON 70

Midas took one of the hotcakes and had scarcely broken it 11
when it turned yellow. If it had been an ordinary white hotcake, 23
Midas would have prized it a good deal more than he now did. 36
Almost in despair, he helped himself to a boiled egg, which 47
immediately changed the same way the fish and hotcake had 57
changed. 58

"Well, this is a problem," he thought, leaning back in his 69
chair and looking with envy at Marygold as she ate her bread and 82
milk with great satisfaction. Midas said to himself, "My breakfast is 93
quite valuable, but I cannot eat it." 100

And truly Midas was a person that you should pity. Here was 112
the richest breakfast that could be set before a king, but its 124
richness was worth absolutely nothing to Midas. The poorest 133
farmer, sitting down to his crust of bread and cup of water, was far 147
better off than King Midas, although the fine food that Midas had 159
before him was worth its weight in gold. And what was he to do? 173
Already, Midas was extremely hungry. How would he feel by 183
dinnertime? And how many days could he survive on golden 193
food? 194

Midas's hunger and despair were so great that he groaned 204
aloud and very sadly, too. Marygold could endure it no longer. She 216
gazed at her father a moment to discover what was the matter 228
with him. Then, with a sweet and sorrowful desire to comfort him, 240
she started from her chair. She ran to Midas, and threw her arms 253
about him. He bent down and kissed her. At that moment, he felt 266
that his little daughter's love was worth a thousand times more 277
than the Golden Touch. 281

Beauty and her father had hardly finished their meal when they | 11
heard the Beast approaching. Beauty clung to her father in terror, | 22
which became all the greater when she saw how frightened he | 33
was. But when the Beast appeared, Beauty made a great effort to | 45
hide her terror. She bowed to him respectfully and thanked him for | 57
his hospitality. | 59

Her behavior seemed to please the Beast. After looking at | 69
her, he said, in a tone that might have struck terror in the boldest | 83
heart, "Good evening, sir. Good evening, Beauty." | 90

The merchant was too terrified to reply, but Beauty answered | 100
sweetly, "Good evening, Beast." | 104

"Have you come willingly?" asked the Beast. "Will you be | 114
content to stay here when your father goes away?" | 123

Beauty answered bravely that she was quite prepared to | 132
stay. | 133

"I am pleased with you," said the Beast. "You seem to have | 145
come of your own choice, so you may stay. As for you, sir," he | 159
added, turning to the merchant, "at sunrise tomorrow you will | 169
leave. When the bell rings, get up and eat your breakfast. You will | 182
find the same horse waiting to take you home. But remember that | 194
you must never expect to see my palace again." | 203

LESSON 90

One day showed just what a fierce competitor Robinson was. **10**
There was a baseball game scheduled in one city and a track **22**
meet in a city forty miles away. These events were scheduled at **34**
the same time, and Robinson was on both the baseball team and **46**
the track team. The track coach asked which sporting event he **57**
wanted to compete in. Robinson said, "Both." And he did **67**
compete in both. **70**

The track coach arranged for Robinson to compete in the **80**
long jump early, before the other events. The idea was for **91**
Robinson to compete in the long jump, get into a waiting car, be **104**
driven forty miles, and play in the baseball game, which would **115**
already be under way. So Robinson did his first long jump. It was a **129**
good jump, a little over twenty-three feet. That was enough to win **141**
the event. **143**

But Robinson wasn't satisfied. He said, "I can do better than **154**
that." So he jumped again. The second jump was more than a foot **167**
farther than the first. **171**

The driver who was taking Robinson to the baseball game **181**
said, "Fantastic. Now let's get out of here." **189**

Robinson shook his head and said, "I can do better than **200**
that." So he went for his third try. And what do you think? He **214**
jumped twenty-five feet, six and a half inches—more than half a **226**
foot farther than the record set by his brother Mack. **236**

Finally Robinson darted off the field, jumped into the car, and **247**
changed into his baseball uniform on the way to the game. There **259**
were only five innings left by the time they got there, but Robinson **272**
still managed to get two hits and help his team to a victory. **285**

LESSON 100

In London, during the year 1537, two boys were born on the same day. One boy was born to a poor family named Canty. This family did not want their boy. The other boy was born to a rich family named Tudor. This family did want their boy. In fact, everybody in England wanted him so much that they were nearly crazy with joy when he was born.

People took holidays to celebrate the birth of the Tudor boy, and they hugged people they scarcely knew. They feasted and danced and sang for days and days. And they talked and talked about the Tudor baby. For, you see, the Tudor baby was a prince— Edward Tudor, Prince of Wales, who lay wrapped in silk, with lords and ladies watching over him.

But there was no talk about the other baby, Tom Canty, who was wrapped in rags. The only people who discussed this baby were those in his family. They weren't happy about little Tom, because they were paupers, and the presence of the baby meant more work and less food for them.

When Tom Canty grew old enough, he became a beggar. He and his family lived in a small, dilapidated house near Pudding Lane. The house was packed full of terribly poor families. Tom's family occupied a room on the third floor. His mother and father slept in a bed in a corner of the room. But Tom, his grandmother and his twin sisters, Bet and Nan, did not have beds. Instead, they slept on the floor in any place they chose. They covered themselves with the old remains of blankets or some bundles of ancient, dirty straw.

12
25
39
50
61
68
79
89
101
114
126
131
143
154
165
176
183
194
205
216
228
242
255
266
277
280

LESSON 110

A man stood up and stripped away some of his rags. He   12
showed his back, which was crisscrossed with thick old scars left   23
by a whip. There was also a large V that had been branded on his   38
shoulder.   39

The man said, "I am Yokel. Once I was a farmer who   51
prospered. I had a loving wife and children. You can see that I'm   64
different now. My wife and children are gone. They're lucky   74
because they don't have to live in England any more. My mother   86
tried to earn a little bread by nursing the sick. One of the people   100
she nursed died, and the doctors did not know why. So they put   113
her in prison."   116

Yokel shook his head and yelled loudly, "English law! Let's   126
cheer for that fine English law!" His voice was bitter as he   138
continued. "After I could not farm, I started to beg. But you know   151
it's against English law to beg. My wife and I went from house to   165
house with our hungry children until they caught us. They lashed   176
us through three towns. Another cheer for English law!"   185

Yokel continued. "My wife died after the last lashing, and my   196
children starved. Those children never harmed any creature, but   205
now they are gone. Then I begged again, just for a crust of bread.   219
When they caught me, I was sold for a slave. A slave! Do you   233
understand that word? I am an English slave, and when I'm found,   241
I shall hang. Another cheer for English law!"   253

As night approached, Edward found himself wandering through   8
a dark and poor part of the city. His feet were so sore that he   23
could hardly walk. As he slowly limped along, he thought of where   35
he would find shelter for the night. He thought back to the   47
questions he had asked Tom and how Tom had answered. He   58
asked himself, "What was the name of that lane near Tom's   69
house?" In a moment, he remembered.   75

A plan formed in his mind. "If I can find Tom's place, I will   89
explain the situation to his parents. They will take me back to the   102
palace and prove I am not Tom but the Prince of Wales."   114

The lights began to twinkle in the houses as people lit their   126
lamps. Now came a heavy rain, blown by a raw wind. Edward   138
moved on slowly through the disgusting alleys where people lived   148
in hives of poverty and misery.   154

Suddenly, a large man grabbed Edward by the collar and   164
said, "Here you are out at night again, and you haven't brought a   177
thing home for me and your poor mother, not even a crust of   190
bread."   191

Edward twisted himself loose and began to brush himself   200
off. "So you are Tom's father," he said. "I'm so glad I found you.   214
We must go back to the palace so you can pick him up and I can   230
once again take up my duties as prince."   238

John Canty slowly shook his finger at Edward. "Don't you   248
play those games with me, Tom Canty, or you'll be one sorry boy."   261

Interpreting Test Results

The test results are recorded on the Individual Skills Profile Chart, the Group Point Chart, and the Writing Assessment Chart. Each chart gives a different interpretation of the results. The Individual Skills Profile Chart shows the specific skills the students have mastered; the Group Point Chart shows the group's overall performance; the Writing Assessment Chart gives students a place to record their writing scores.

The Individual Skills Profile Chart

The Individual Skills Profile Chart should be used to assess each student's strengths and weaknesses. Test items the student missed on an initial test will be circled; items missed on a retest will be crossed out. On the sample chart below, the student took a retest on lesson 20. Note that some items have been both circled and crossed out for lesson 20.

If a chart has a great many items that are circled or crossed out, the student may still be weak in certain areas. Look for two general patterns of weakness. In the first pattern, a student will consistently fail items that measure a particular skill. On the sample chart below, for example, the student consistently failed items that measured the skill "inferring causes and effects." Students who fall into this pattern may require further teaching of particular skills.

In the second pattern, a student will do poorly on one test but fairly well on the other tests. On the sample chart below, for example, the student did poorly on the test for lesson 20. Usually, students who fall into this pattern were absent on the days preceding the test. These students may profit from a review of the lessons they missed.

Individual Skills Profile Chart A   Name: **Sample**

	Skills	Tests	10	20	30	40	50	60
Comprehension Skills	using vocabulary words in context		1, 2, 3	1, 2, 3	1, 2 / 3, 4 / 5, 6	1, 2, 3	1, 2, 3	1, 2 / 3, 4 / 5, 6
	using context to predict word meaning		4, 5, 6	4, 5, (6)	7, 8 / 9, 10 / 11, 12	4, 5, 6	4, 5, 6	7, 8 / 9, 10 / 11, 12
	answering literal questions about a text		13		17, 44	15	16	22, 34
	identifying literal cause and effect		7		14, 34	13		21, 26
	recalling details and events				13, 22, 36	7	11	28, 40
	sequencing narrative events		9		15, 35			36, 44
	predicting narrative outcomes		16		18, (47)	14	15	24, 45
	relating titles to story content		18	13	26, 45			38, 43
	inferring causes and effects		(14)	(✗)	19, (28), 30		(13)	14, (35)
	inferring story details and events				43	14		15, (41)
	making comparisons			15	24, 31		9	13, 42
	inferring the main idea						7	27, 49, 48
	drawing conclusions			(✗)	48	9		20, 46
	evaluating problems and solutions		(15)		21	8		19, 50
Literary Skills	interpreting a character's feelings		10	18	20, 33		17	32, 51
	interpreting a character's motives			7	(32), 46	10	18	(33), 37
	inferring a character's point of view			17	27	18		23
	predicting a character's actions		17		29	17		16, 53
	distinguishing settings by features		8	8, (11)	16, 37		10	31
	distinguishing characters by trait			(9), 10	25, 38	16	12	25, 39, 52
	distinguishing between fact and fiction			12	42		(8)	47
Study Skills	interpreting maps		11, 12		39, 40			29, 30
	interpreting glossaries				23, 41			
	interpreting indexes and headings					11, 12		17, 18
	Total		**16**	**13**	**45**	**18**	**16**	**50**
	Retest			✗				
	FINAL SCORE		**16**	**16**	**45**	**18**	**16**	**50**

Individual Skills Profile Chart A

Name _____

Skills	Tests	10	20	30	40	50	60
Comprehension Skills	using vocabulary words in context	1 2 3	1 2 3	1, 2, 3, 4, 5, 6	1 2 3	1 2 3	1, 2, 3, 4, 5, 6
	using context to predict word meaning	4 5 6	4 5 6	7, 8, 9, 10, 11, 12	4 5 6	4 5 6	7, 8, 9, 10, 11, 12
	answering literal questions about a text	13		17 44	15	16	22 34
	identifying literal cause and effect	7		14, 34	13		21, 26
	recalling details and events			13, 22, 36	7	11	28, 40
	sequencing narrative events	9		15, 35			36, 44
	predicting narrative outcomes	16		18, 47	14	15	24, 45
	relating titles to story content	18	13	26, 45			38, 43
	inferring causes and effects	14	14	19, 28, 30		13	14 35
	inferring story details and events			43		14	15, 41
	making comparisons		15	24, 31		9	13, 42
	inferring the main idea					7	27, 48, 49
	drawing conclusions		16	48	9		20, 46
	evaluating problems and solutions	15		21	8		19, 50
Literary Skills	interpreting a character's feelings	10	18	20, 33		17	32, 51
	interpreting a character's motives		7	32, 46	10	18	33, 37
	inferring a character's point of view		17	27	18		23
	predicting a character's actions	17		29	17		16, 53
	distinguishing settings by features	8	8, 11	16, 37		10	31
	distinguishing characters by trait		9 10	25 38	16	12	25, 39, 52
	distinguishing between fact and fiction		12	42		8	47
Study Skills	interpreting maps	11, 12		39, 40			29, 30
	interpreting glossaries			23, 41			
	interpreting indexes and headings				11, 12		17, 18
	Total						
	Retest						
	FINAL SCORE						

Individual Skills Profile Chart B

Name _____

	Skills / Tests	70	80	90	100	110	120
Comprehension Skills	using vocabulary words in context	1, 2, 3, 4, 5, 6	1, 2, 3, 4	1, 2, 3, 4	1, 2, 3, 4, 5, 6	1, 2, 3, 4	1, 2, 3, 4
	using context to predict word meaning	5, 6, 7, 8	5, 6, 7, 8	7, 8, 9, 10, 11, 12	5, 6, 7, 8	5, 6, 7, 8	7, 8, 9, 10, 11, 12
	answering literal questions about a text			19 31	23	18	21, 31, 32
	identifying literal cause and effect	21	15	14, 49	9	11	14
	recalling details and events	9		38	11	13	39
	sequencing narrative events		11	13	12	12	13, 30, 47
	predicting narrative outcomes			36, 51		14	48
	relating titles to story content		22	23, 52			36
	inferring causes and effects		20	28 37	18	17	22, 34, 42
	inferring story details and events	17		16, 32, 48	13	19	17 46
	making comparisons	10	14	42	20		29, 38
	inferring the main idea	12	18, 19	21, 29	15	15	19, 40
	inferring details relevant to a main idea			22 30	16	16	20 41
	drawing conclusions		13 21	25, 41, 53	19	9	37
	evaluating problems and solutions	18		33, 39		23	
Literary Skills	interpreting a character's feelings	22		17 34	14	20	16, 33, 44
	interpreting a character's motives		12	20, 35		22	27, 43
	inferring a character's point of view	20		15 43	21		15, 24, 28
	predicting a character's actions	19	23	24		21	23, 45
	distinguishing settings by features		9	27, 50	22	10	26, 35
	distinguishing characters by trait	11	10	26, 40	10		25
	distinguishing between fact and fiction		17	18			
Study Skills	interpreting maps	15, 16		44, 45			
	interpreting time lines	13, 14		46, 47			
	interpreting indexes and headings		16		17		18
	Total						
	Retest						
	FINAL SCORE						

Mastery Test Group Summary Chart A

Assessment	10	20	30	40	50	60
Number of assessment items	16	16	48	17	17	53

Notes for recording:

- Write student names in left-hand column.
- Record percent of items correct on each assessment and highlight a score below 80%.
- Provide remediation to students with a score below 80%.

Mastery Test Group Summary Chart B

Assessment	70	80	90	100	110	120
Number of assessment items	23	24	53	23	24	49

Notes for recording:

- Write student names in left-hand column.
- Record percent of items correct on each assessment and highlight a score below 80%.
- Provide remediation to students with a score below 80%.

Reading Mastery Grade 4

Individual Fluency: Rate/Accuracy Chart

Student performance should be recorded as total time over number of errors.

Names	After Lesson Time/ #errors	10 1:00/ 2	20 1:00/ 2	30 1:00/ 2	40 1:00/ 2	50 1:00/ 2	60 1:00/ 2	70 1:00/ 2	80 1:00/ 2	90 1:00/ 2	100 1:00/ 2	110 1:00/ 2	120 1:00/ 2
Retest													
Retest													
Retest													
Retest													
Retest													
Retest													
Retest													
Retest													
Retest													
Retest													

Writing Assessment Chart

Name _____

Test	Score	Ways to Improve
10		
20		
30		
40		
50		
60		
70		
80		
90		
100		
110		
120		

Placement Test

PART 1

An Underwater World

The diving boat was anchored in a place where the water changed from light green to dark, dark blue. One by one, the divers went down the ladder on the side of the boat and entered the warm water. The boat was about 1,600 kilometers east of Florida. They were south of the Bermuda Islands. Darla was the last diver to go down the ladder and enter the warm water.

"Now stick together," the guide said as he floated with his mask tilted back on his forehead. "You've got your partners. Stay with your partner. If you see something you want to look at, signal me. If one person stops, we all stop or somebody's going to get lost."

The guide continued, "If you get separated, go to the surface of the water. Don't try to look for the rest of us. Just go to the surface. And remember, don't go up too fast. Take at least two minutes to go up, or you may get the bends."

The bends. Darla had read about the bends. She knew that a person gets them because of the great pressure of the water.

PART 2

1. Near which islands does this story take place?

   _____

2. Why was the group in this place?

   _____

3. Was the water warm or cold?

   _____

4. Who led the group?

   _____

5. Each diver was supposed to stay with a

   _____

6. What was a diver supposed to do if the diver wanted to stop to examine something?

   _____

7. What was a diver supposed to do if the diver got separated from the group?

   _____

8. What problem would the diver have if the diver went up to the surface too fast?

   _____

9. This problem was caused by the great _____ of the water.